INTO
OUTER SPACE

INTO
OUTER SPACE

David Owen

ROXBURY PARK

LOWELL HOUSE
LOS ANGELES
NTC/Contemporary Publishing Group

Published by Lowell House
A division of NTC/Contemporary Publishing Group, Inc.
4255 West Touhy Avenue, Lincolnwood (Chicago),
Illinois 60712-1975 U.S.A.

Library of Congress Cataloging-in-Publication Data
Owen, David, 1939-
        Into Outer Space: an exploration of man's obsession with the cosmos: fact and fiction/
David Owen
        p.cm.
    Includes index.
    ISBN 0-7373-0469-3
        1.Astronautics–History. 2.Outer space–Exploration–History. I.Title.
    TL788.5 .O94 2000
    910'.919–dc21

                            00-026964

Lowell House books can be purchased at special discounts when ordered in bulk for premiums and
special sales. Contact Department SC at the following address:
NTC/Contemporary Publishing Group
4255 West Touhy Avenue
Lincolnwood, IL 60712-1975
1-800-323-4900

ISBN: 0-7373-0469-3

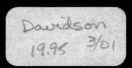

Roxbury Park is a division of NTC/Contemporary Publishing Group, Inc.

Managing Director and Publisher: Jack Artenstein
Editor in chief, Roxbury Park Books: Michael Artenstein
Director of Publishing Services: Rena Copperman
Director of Art Production: Bret Perry
Editorial Assistant: Nicole Monastirsky

Conceived, designed and produced by
Quintet Publishing Limited
6 Blundell Street
London N7 7BH

Senior Project Editor: Toria Leitch
Art Director: Simon Daley
Copy Editor: Daisy Leitch
Designers: James Lawrence, Noam Toran
Creative Director: Richard Dewing
Publisher: Oliver Salzmann

Typeset in Great Britain by
Central Southern Typesetters, Eastbourne

Manufactured by Regent Publishing Services Limited, Hong Kong
Printed by Leefung-Asco Printers Ltd, China.

CONTENTS

THE MAPPING
OF SPACE

The work of the pioneer astronomers in laying

the foundations for understanding the heavens

has enabled us to send spacecraft to distant

planets and enable human beings to stand on the

surface of the Moon.

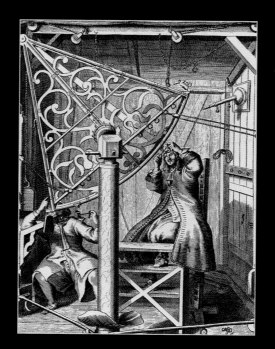

From long before the dawn of recorded history, human beings marveled at the stupendous spectacle of the starlit sky, with no understanding of the colossal complexity and size of the universe. Ancient civilizations saw pictures in groups of stars or constellations, and named them after gods or heroes. The Babylonians predicted planetary movements by calculations, the Mayans of Mexico and Central America studied the stars to determine the times for planting and harvesting, and one theory suggests the monument of Stonehenge is an elaborate astronomical computer.

Some two thousand years ago, the true science of astronomy began to develop in the work of pioneers like Claudius Ptolemy, a Greek working in Alexandria around AD 150. His original writings were lost in the Dark Ages that followed the collapse of the Roman Empire, and his work only survived because it had been copied by Arab scholars and then later retranslated.

Ptolemy's map of the heavens was derived from what he could see with his unaided eye. Apart from the distant stars that appeared perfectly fixed in their positions, the objects that moved were the Sun and the Moon, and

starlike objects that were actually the closest planets to Earth in the solar system. Ptolemy explained these movements by assuming that Earth was stationary, and that the Sun, the Moon, and the planets all revolved around it on circular orbits (see opposite).

Ptolemy's basic assumptions were wrong, though it would be centuries before the errors were revealed. For the time being, his theory seemed to explain the movements of the planets, and this knowledge allowed the spread of Islam across the world. For a devout Muslim, it was essential to know the direction of Mecca, and the time of sunrise and sunset when hundreds of miles from the holy places so that prayers could be said according to the Koran. With an astrolabe to measure the height of the Sun or a particular star over the horizon and the aid of a star map, it was possible to determine all these things through careful and complex calculations.

Soon astronomy became more widely useful, as fixed stars helped guide navigators at sea without earthbound landmarks. The position of the Pole Star indicated true north as long as the nights were clear to enable it to

Far right Italian astronomer and physicist Galileo Galilei (1564–1642).
Below right Tycho Brahe (1546–1601), taken from *Tycho Brahe Opera*, Vol IV, 1596.

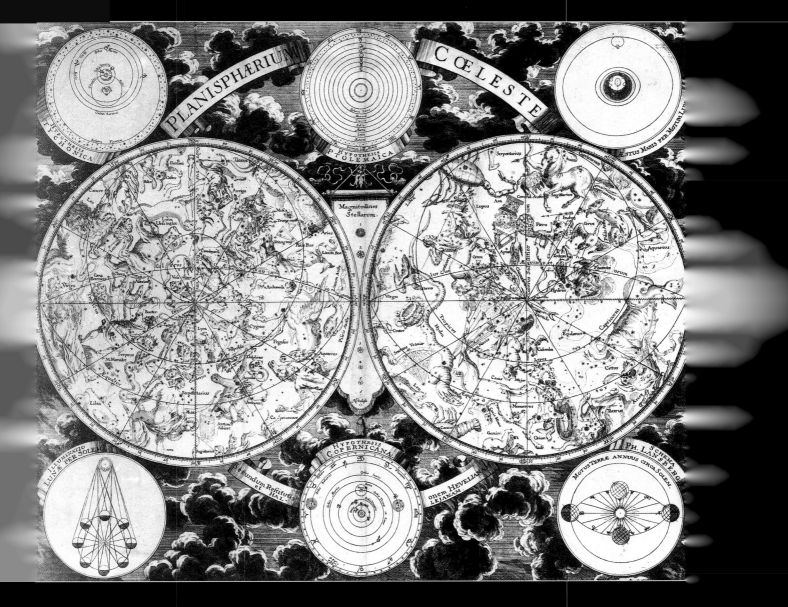

Ptolemy and other Greek astronomers were prisoners of their own philosophy. Because they did not understand the concept of gravity, they believed Earth must be stationary in space at the center of the universe, otherwise, they reasoned, everything would be swept off its surface by its movement. Since they also believed that heavenly bodies must obey perfect rules, and because they believed that the only perfect motion was circular, they held the conviction that all the planets must move in circular orbits. However, even though their observations of the visible universe were effectively limited to the six inner planets of

the solar system, the motion of these planets could not be explained simply by adopting a series of concentric orbits around the Sun.

The only way the Ptolemy system could be made to work at all, even within the accuracy of the measurements and observations that could be made at the time, was to assume that each planet followed a circular path, not around Earth itself, but around a circle around Earth called a deferent. This idea of a circular orbit around part of a circular orbit led to complex and unwieldy mathematics, but it was the only way to reconcile their different assumptions.

Above Illustrations of var celestial planispheres, in those of Ptolemy, Tycho and Copernicus.

be seen. Only later would more precise instruments, such as the sextant, and the printing of tables allow the positions of the stars in the heavens to indicate the latitude of a ship's position on a long voyage across a featureless ocean.

The biggest step forward in understanding the heavens came in 1609, when a group of Dutch inventors came to the wealthy trading city of Venice in Italy with a prototype spy-glass with which to view distant objects in detail. Working in the city at the time was a scientist and mathematical professor from Padua named Galileo Galilei, who saw the advantages of such a device. Without even seeing the new invention, he worked out its principles and constructed his own glass, which magnified distant images about three times. But this was merely the beginning. He strove to improve it, with the result that he stepped up the magnification to a factor of eight or more, then persuaded the senate of the city to climb to the top of the campanile in Saint Mark's Square for a demonstration.

This telescope enabled the Venetian merchants to identify their ships as they approached the harbor and thereby gain a lead over competitors. Galileo had a completely different objective. He modified his telescope again and again, boosting its magnification to a factor of thirty in a matter of months. Then he turned it skyward to use its power to unravel the secrets of the heavens and answer a series of increasingly difficult questions that were perplexing the scientists of the time.

Sixty-six years before, a Polish priest and mathematician, named Copernicus (or Niklas Koppernigk), had first cast doubt on Ptolemy's map of the universe. He had seen strange anomalies in the motions of the planets, which Ptolemy's ideas could not explain. He was also convinced that the power and majesty of the Sun meant that it, and not Earth, must be at the center of the universe. He proposed a completely different system, placing Earth and all the other planets, rotating in circular orbits, about the Sun. This correction to a simplistic picture was seen at the time as heresy, and it was to bring the views of Copernicus and his followers into head-on conflict with the Church.

Worse was to come. Late in the year 1572, a new star appeared in the constellation of Cassiopeia, a star blazing so brightly that it could be seen in the daytime. It shone with undiminished brilliance for two years before fading away into darkness. This was a nova, although noone understood this at the time. Yet *what* it was proved to be less important than *where* it was.

A twenty-six-year old Danish astronomer named Tycho Brahe had developed instruments that could measure the positions of stars with greater accuracy than ever before. When the position of the new star was measured from a number of different points, the consistency of the results showed that it must be a colossal distance from Earth. For the first time, astronomers began to suspect how enormous the universe was. Brahe, however, was suspicious of anomalies in the movement of the planets that even Copernicus's map could not explain.

Brahe proposed that the real situation was that all the planets, except Earth, were in orbit around the Sun, which was itself in orbit

Below Hand-colored engraving showing Copernicus's planetary system, issued in Paris in 1761.

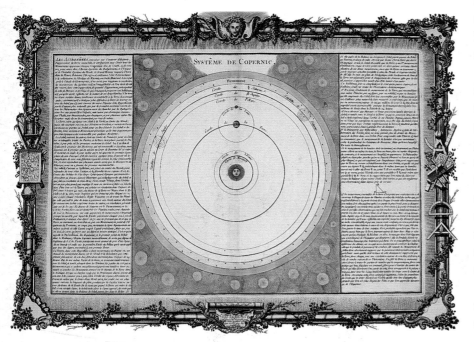

COPERNICUS, BRAHE, AND KEPLER'S VIEW OF THE HEAVENS

Copernicus shared Ptolemy's view that the planets moved in perfectly circular orbits, but around the Sun rather than Earth. This produced a system that was much closer to the observations of astronomers, as it explained the movement of Mars and Venus. Measurements of the paths of these planets had produced results that had been totally at variance with Ptolemy's system. Copernicus also included the distant stars in his plan of the universe, but simply assumed that these did not move at all and were set around the surface of a sphere in space, at equal distances from the Sun as center of the universe.

Since there were still discrepancies between Copernicus's plan of the universe and what astronomers could see and measure for themselves with the unaided eye, Tycho Brahe proposed a compromise between the two earlier systems. In Brahe's plan, all the planets except Earth did indeed orbit the Sun on circular paths, but the Sun was assumed to follow a circular path around Earth, which remained center of the universe.

Johannes Kepler made the final step in understanding how the planets revolved around the Sun. He agreed with Copernicus that all the planets of the solar system did indeed orbit the Sun, but by careful measurements and calculations he showed that their paths in space were not circular but elliptical. In time, Galileo came to the same conclusion by studying the movement of Venus through his powerful telescope.

Above Tycho Brahe's Mural Quadrant, 1602, from *Astronomiae Instauratae Mechanicæ*.

around Earth, together with the Moon. This idea was accepted at the time, but Johannes Kepler, a young German who taught mathematics and astronomy in Graz, was to prove it wrong. He became Brahe's assistant in 1600, when the Dane had been appointed royal astronomer to the Austrian Imperial Court. When Brahe died two years later, Kepler was left with his paperwork, his calculations, and the time to study them closely.

Kepler became obsessed with the differences between the way in which the planets *should* move, according to Brahe's calculations, and how his own observations showed they *did* move. In particular, the orbit of the planet Mars could not be explained by either Copernicus or Brahe. This was measurably longer on one side of the Sun than it was on the other, and after studying the problem for four years and preparing 900 pages of calculation, Kepler concluded that the pioneer astronomers were wrong. The planets did not move in circular orbits but in elliptical ones. Calculations based on that assumption, and his own observations, indicated the length of a planet's orbit around the Sun was proportional to its distance around the Sun. For the first time, the laws governing planetary motion were being expressed in accurate mathematical terms, an enormous step forward in understanding how the universe worked.

Not long after Kepler's findings, Galileo began to explore the night skies, reveling in the size and detail of the images provided by his powerful telescope. He saw vast numbers of previously invisible stars, some of them grouped together in what he called "clouds" or "nebulae." He scanned the surface of the Moon and its craters and mountain ranges. But when he turned to the largest planet of the solar system, Jupiter, he found something much more astonishing, which was eventually to threaten his very freedom.

NICOLAVS COPERNICVS
Mathematicus.

Above Woodcut of Copernicus (1473–1543).
Above right Johannes Kepler, (1571–1630).
Right and far right Sketches of the moon from Galileo's *Sidereus Nuncius*, 1610.

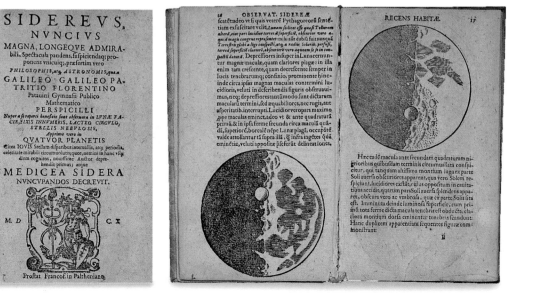

Close to the huge planet he saw four new stars, two to the east and two to the west of Jupiter. When he looked again the following night, he expected that the movement of Jupiter against the apparently static stars beyond would have resulted in all four of these stars being to the east of the planet, but they were not. All four were to the *west*. After a series of careful observations, Galileo came to the staggering conclusion that these were not stars at all, but small planets or moons, which were in orbit around Jupiter, like the Moon circling Earth.

This had very dramatic implications. If Jupiter could have four satellites and still orbit around the Sun, why should Earth and its one satellite not do the same? Galileo went on to study the planet Venus, which he could clearly see in its different phases as it circled in orbit around the Sun. All these observations were reinforcing Copernicus' and Kepler's explanation of the relationship between the planets, as they orbited around the Sun at different distances from it.

Galileo produced two famous papers in 1610 and 1632, which reinforced the theories of Copernicus, cutting straight across the teaching of the Church. In 1633, he was put on trial in Rome by the Holy Office of the Inquisition, who had been watching his work and preparing their case since the appearance of his first paper more than twenty years before. Threatened with torture, as a result of the court's findings, he was forced to recant and repudiate all his work. He was placed under house arrest and forbidden to discuss or publish anything at all relating to astronomy.

Galileo died nine years later, still confined to his house, and his papers remained on the banned list for more than two centuries, meaning that all Catholics were forbidden to read them. But he and his fellow pioneers, by careful observation and clear thinking, had laid the foundations for understanding the heavens, which in time would allow spacecraft to travel to the distant planets and enable human beings to stand on the surface of the Moon.

Tools of the astronomer's trade— refracting and reflecting telescopes

The telescopes used by both Galileo and Kepler were refracting telescopes, which used a double lens to produce their magnified images. In Galileo's case, he matched a concave lens with a convex magnifying lens in a tube. The first lens was the object lens, which focused light from distant planets onto the second lens, the eye lens, which magnified the resulting image. A year after Galileo produced his first telescope, Kepler produced an improved version by using two convex magnifying lenses that gave a wider field of vision and produced clearer images than Galileo's instrument.

The limiting factor of early refracting telescopes was the quality of their lenses, which tended to break up white light into a spectrum of colors. Sir Isaac Newton designed a telescope that avoided this break up by using a curved mirror to collect the light and deflect it into a magnifying eyepiece instead of a lens. This was the first reflecting telescope, and these soon came to dominate the field. Even when better-quality lenses made refracting telescopes more efficient, the relative compactness of reflecting telescopes, together with the fact that it was easier to support very large mirrors than equally large lenses, enabled them to maintain their supremacy. The largest reflecting telescopes are the Mount Palomar telescope in California with a 200 inch (5 meter) diameter mirror, and the Zelenchukskaya telescope in the Caucasus with a 240 inch (6 meter) diameter mirror.

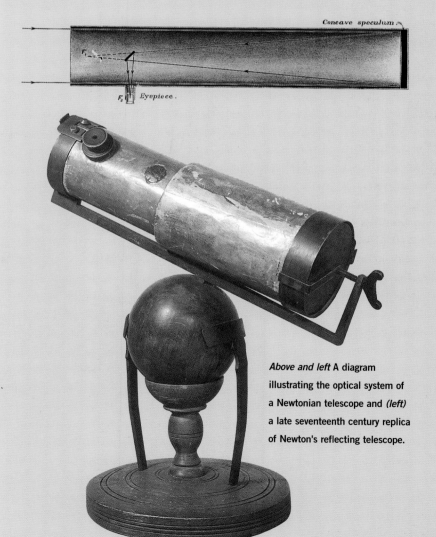

Above and left A diagram illustrating the optical system of a Newtonian telescope and *(left)* a late seventeenth century replica of Newton's reflecting telescope.

TO THE FURTHEST REACHES—
OBSERVATIONS BY RADIO TELESCOPE

Below Arecibo Observatory antenna at the National Astronomy and Ionosphere Center in Puerto Rico.

Ever since the invention of the camera, optical telescopes have been able to extend their reach further into the universe, by using film to collect light over a long period and reveal the presence of stars that would otherwise be invisible to human observers. A method of "seeing" even further was first discovered in the 1930s by an American communications engineer called Karl Jansky, who was searching for the source of noise on radio-telephone channels when he recorded radio waves coming to Earth from space.

These radio waves cover a longer distance than does visible light, and so can reveal the presence of stars and galaxies far beyond the range of optical telescopes. Because their

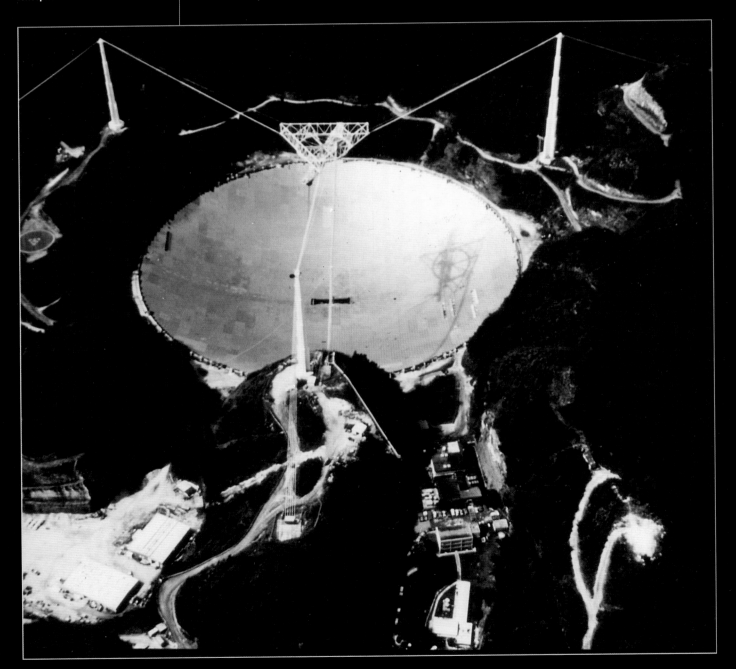

wavelength is so much longer than that of
visible light, they need to be focused and
recorded by much larger telescopes. At first,
these were built as large, steerable dishes
which performed the same function as the
reflecting mirror of an optical telescope. The
pioneer U.K. radio telescope at Jodrell Bank
in Cheshire, England, was a dish so large that
it was rotated by a mechanism that had once
directed the gun turret of a battleship.

   The largest single-dish radio telescope was
built at Arecibo in the mountains of Puerto
Rico in the Caribbean in 1963, with a fixed
dish 1,000 feet (305 meters) across. In more
recent years, computers have enabled
astronomers to combine signals from linked
radio telescopes to produce the equivalent
picture to that of a much larger dish. The
Very Large Array telescope in New Mexico
was built in the early 1980s, and produces an
image equivalent to that generated by a dish
17 miles (27 kilometers) across.

COSMIC CLOCKWORK: THE LAWS OF SPACE & HOW THE UNIVERSE WORKS

As Newton's laws of motion began to explain the movement of the planets, it seemed that space travel was becoming ever closer to reality.

Above Sir Isaac Newton
(1642–1727).

Above Leon Foucault
(1819–1868).

Kepler's careful observations of planetary movements had shown that the length of a planet's orbit was proportional to its distance from the Sun. He also suggested that there must be a force between Earth and the Moon to hold the satellite in orbit, relative to the mass of both planets and which caused the formation of the tides. What he had not explained was how it was possible for Earth to move through space without this being obvious to anyone standing on its surface. This was left to the brilliant mathematician Sir Isaac Newton, a young graduate from Cambridge University.

In 1665, Newton was twenty-three years old when the Great Plague from London, England, reached the university. To escape the danger of infection, he moved back to his birthplace at Woolsthorp in Lincolnshire, and remained there for two years, working on his mathematical research. By the time he returned to the university, he had worked out how the universe worked, though he would not publish his findings for another two decades.

Newton suggested that all objects attract other objects relative to their size. A person standing on the surface of Earth is held to Earth by gravity, but the person's mass also attracts Earth by an immeasurably small amount. Furthermore, since the gravity of Earth also holds the atmosphere in place, there is no sensation of Earth's movement through space at its surface. Earth, the atmosphere, and everything on its surface are all moving through space at exactly the same velocity. The only signs of movement are the Sun's path across the heavens by day, and the rotation of the stars about the Pole Star at night, caused by Earth rotating on its own axis, rather than orbiting the Sun.

Newton went further. He drew up his three Laws of Motion, which between them explained all planetary movements. His first law stated that any immobile body will either remain at rest in the same position, or will continue its motion in a straight line, unless acted on by an outside force. His second law stated that the action of an outside force on a body will make it accelerate in the direction of the force, by an amount proportional to the size of the force. His third law then went on to state that every action has an equal and opposite reaction.

Newton showed that every body attracts any other body with a force directly proportional to the result of their masses multiplied together, and inversely proportional to the square of the distance between them. This explained why the Moon stayed in orbit around Earth, for example. Newton's first law showed its natural tendency was to move in a straight line, but this was balanced by the gravity between Earth and the Moon that forced it to follow a regular orbit around the planet.

Newton's laws explained how and why the planets move in their orbits around the Sun. Moreover, his concept of gravity was eventually able to explain how the trajectory of a spacecraft could be controlled to follow a desired path through the gravitational fields of different planets to navigate across the solar system and into deeper space.

Newton published his findings in his *Principia Mathematica* in 1687, and since then his findings have held true for any calculations involving a fixed frame of reference. For this reason, Newton's laws are still vital in space exploration, although later scientists like Einstein, with his general and special theories of relativity (see p. 21) have examined the anomalies caused by multiple frames of reference, and the finite speed of light.

Thirty-two years after Newton published his master work, a French physicist called Pierre Bouguer was able to find evidence to reinforce his theory of gravity. Bouguer reasoned that if Newton was right, the mass of a mountain ought to exert enough gravitational force to deflect a plumb line from hanging vertically downward. When the experiment was tried, the small but genuine deflection was measured. Not only had Newton's theory been right, but his

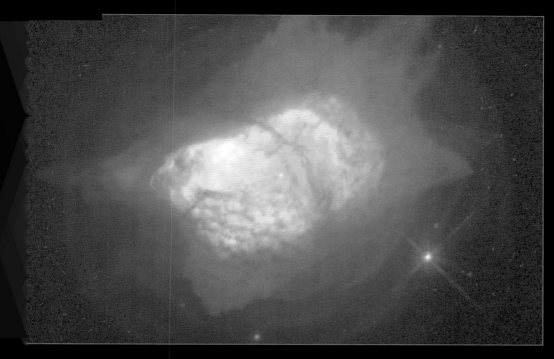

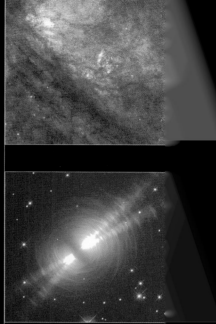

Stars are born from huge clouds of dust and gas within the galaxies. As a cloud shrinks under the gravitational forces of the particles from which it is made, some areas will become denser than others. These collapse into globules of matter that form the future stars, and as the particles collide with one another at an increasing rate, the resulting friction causes this matter to glow hotter and hotter. Eventually, after perhaps millions of years, the temperature rises to the point where nuclear reactions begin.

Most of the atoms of matter in the growing star are hydrogen atoms, and the enormous pressures and temperatures convert these to helium, in a similar reaction to the explosion of a hydrogen bomb. Once this reaction reaches a stable level, the star can go on burning as a thermonuclear furnace for thousands of millions of years. How long this stable stage lasts depends on the size of the star, as larger stars burn more fiercely and more quickly than smaller ones.

The smallest stars never achieve a fierce enough reaction to burn with the brightness of the Sun, and their small size and dull glow earns them the name of red dwarfs, which

continue burning for millions of millions of years. The life of larger stars is limited when the reserves of unburned hydrogen at the core begin to run out. The fiercest reactions move outward from the center to the outer layers of the star, where hydrogen reserves still exist.

The star grows hotter and larger, to become a red giant. When the Sun reaches this stage, in some 5,000 million years, it will expand to a hundred times its present size, and its output of heat and light energy will increase by a thousandfold. Some smaller stars will then fade away as their final reserves of hydrogen burn out.

Others are large enough for the outer shell of hydrogen gas to continue heating the central core, which is now made up almost entirely of helium. When the temperature and pressure are high enough, another nuclear reaction breaks down the helium atoms, releasing still more energy and converting the core into carbon. This reaction then spreads outward in another red giant stage as the helium is used up. More and more of its matter spreads out into space as the central core cools, turning the star into a white dwarf. Finally the star dies down into a black dwarf of intensely dense ash.

Above left Image of the planetary nebula NGC 7027 showing new details of the process by which a star like the Sun dies.
Top Behind a dusty veil lies a cradle of star birth.
Above Image of the Egg Nebula (CRL2688) showing a pair of "searchlight" beams emerging from a hidden star as part of its death sequence.

Right Foucault's demonstration of Earth's rotation using an extremely long pendulum in the Pantheon, Paris, 1880.

mathematical equations enabled the mass of the mountain to be calculated.

Eight years later, another astronomer, James Bradley, was able to prove that Earth moved through space, by measuring through a telescope an effect called the aberration of starlight. This is an apparent change in the position of a star, due to Earth moving around the Sun, which causes the rays from the star to appear to arrive on a slanting path, rather like raindrops seen from a moving vehicle.

However, the largest step forward in demonstrating the size of the universe beyond the solar system, was taken by the German astronomer Friedrich Bessel, who noticed the apparent change of position of a distant star caused by the movement of Earth around the Sun. By measuring this apparent shift from different points on Earth's orbit, he was able to calculate the distance between Earth, and the star 61 Cygni as approximately 60 million million miles (96 million million kilometers).

Another French physicist, Jean Foucault, showed in 1851 that a progressive creep in the path traced by successive swings of a large pendulum, showed conclusively that Earth was rotating about its own axis. By this time, better-quality telescopes had already revealed the existence of two more outer planets of the solar system; Uranus (identified in 1781) and Neptune (in 1846). The outermost planet, Pluto, was finally discovered in 1930.

With increasing knowledge about the huge distances between the solar systems and even the nearest stars, astronomers now realized the true significance of the Sun, the solar system, and Earth in the cosmic scheme of things. William Herschel, who had first identified the planet Uranus, also studied the densest pattern of stars in the night sky, the Milky Way, which extends as a bright path from horizon to horizon. He suggested this was due to the solar system being part of a much larger group of stars called a galaxy. Furthermore, the appearance of the Milky Way was due to the stars which formed it being part of this same wheel-shaped galaxy.

In 1918, an American astronomer named Harlow Shapley measured the distances of clusters of stars within the galaxy, and used this to calculate the size of the whole galaxy as 100,000 light-years across (see p. 22). Far from being unique, the Sun was outclassed by many more powerful neighbors among the 100,000 million stars within the galaxy. In the 1950s, scientists were able to detect radiation emitted from hydrogen gas within the galaxy that showed it was made up of spiral arms radiating from the center. The Sun and the solar system were located some 30,000 light years out on one of these radiating arms.

By this time, the importance of the Milky Way galaxy within the context of the universe as a whole had been demonstrated by another American astronomer, Edwin Hubble in 1924. Using the huge Mount Wilson telescope to study the Andromeda nebula, he found this was another vast galaxy. He identified whole groups of galaxies, and found that each one was receding from another; proof that the universe is not only vaster than all previous estimates, but is continually expanding.

Hubble's discovery of the fact that the galaxies were moving further and further apart was based on the light they emitted. When this was broken up into a spectrum, he found a curious distortion. Light of a given wavelength was shifted toward the red end of the spectrum, reflecting a lengthening of that wavelength. This could only be caused by the source of the light receding at high speed, in an optical equivalent of the Doppler Shift heard when a moving sound source passes by.

The amount of the red shift revealed the relative speed between the source of the light and Earth. Hubble found that other, more distant galaxies were receding more quickly. His calculations showed the speed was proportional to the distance—a galaxy twice as far away from Earth was receding at double the speed. So exact was this relationship that it amounted to 10.5 miles (17 kilometers) per second for every million light years of distance. This was named Hubble's constant.

Einstein and relativity

In terms of life on Earth, the velocity of light seems almost infinite, and it is safe to assume that we see events as soon as they happen. However, across the enormous gulfs of space, light travels at a relatively slow rate, and this limitation distorts the assumptions of classical physics, as devised by Newton and his peers. Moreover, careful experiments to measure the speed of light in different directions, which classical physics suggested should vary depending on whether it was measured with or against the rotation of Earth, showed it was exactly the same in all directions.

The assumption that the speed of light never changes is the keystone of Albert Einstein's Theories of Relativity, originally developed early in the twentieth century. Einstein showed in the "Special Theory of Relativity" that because the speed of light is a constant, time would pass at different rates depending on the speed of the person measuring it. The closer these speeds to that of light, the more marked the effects on the passing of time.

In the same way, mass and energy can be converted from one to the other. The faster an object travels the greater its energy and its mass, though once again the speeds have to be colossal for this effect to be measurable. Conversely, if matter is converted entirely into energy, as in a nuclear bomb, the amount of energy produced from a relatively small amount of matter is equivalent to millions of tons of conventional explosives.

Einstein went on to develop the general theory of relativity, which showed that the effects of gravity and acceleration are identical. Because light takes a finite time to travel across space, it is distorted by the gravitational fields through which it passes. Since the only truly straight line in space would be the path of a light beam passing through no gravity at all, this must be impossible. Consequently, all lines in space are curved and space itself is often described as curved, since the masses of the stars and planets effectively curve the spaces around them by the gravitational fields they produce.

Right Albert Einstein (1879–1955) lecturing to the American Association for the Advancement of Science at Pittsburgh, U.S.

INTERPLANETARY DISTANCES

The colossal distances of interstellar space become almost meaningless when expressed in millions of millions of miles or kilometers, and astronomers soon realized some much larger unit of measurement was needed to make sense of them. Since the speed of light is some 186,000 miles (300,000 kilometers) per second, then light travels a distance of approximately 5,874,989 million miles (9,460,530 million kilometers) in a normal year. The light year became the almost universal measurement of distances in space, partly because it helps understand the time taken by light to reach Earth from distant objects. In other words, light from a galaxy two million light years distant will have taken two million years to reach an observer on Earth. Consequently, we see that galaxy as it was two million years ago. To see it as it is now, an observer would have to wait another two million years!

More recently, distances have usually been expressed in even larger units called parsecs. Each parsec is a distance so vast that seen from one parsec away the width of Earth's orbit around the Sun (186,000 miles or 300 million kilometers) would appear as an angle of $\frac{1}{360}$ of a degree. Each parsec is equal to 3.26 light years, or 19,170,000 million miles (30,856,000 million kilometers).

Below Images of the six planets in our solar system put together in a composite scene.

The implications of this discovery were staggering. Georges Lemaître, a Belgian astrophysicist, suggested in 1927 that if this movement were reversed, all the galaxies would come together in one spot at the center of the universe. This implied the universe must have begun from what he termed a cosmic egg, by an enormous explosion, accelerating fragments in different directions throughout space. This became known as the big bang theory, and it remains the most favored of the three current theories.

More recently, a rival group of astronomers devised the steady state theory. This suggested that as the galaxies receded from one another, new material was created from interstellar gas to fill the gap, so the structure and the appearance of the Universe never changed. A third theory, the oscillating universe, suggested that in time the vanishing galaxies would be slowed down by gravity, and would plunge back into the center of the

Universe, to trigger a huge explosion and yet another expansion.

For the time being, evidence has been in favor of the big bang theory. Because of the colossal distance of some of the more distant sources of the radiation picked up by radio telescopes, this radiation must have started out on its journey to Earth millions of years ago. When these older radio sources were counted, astronomers found they were more numerous than objects closer to Earth. In other words, the structure of the universe had changed over time, which suggested the steady state theory was wrong.

Additional reinforcement for the big bang theory came from the discovery, in 1965, of low-energy radiation. This showed that space was very slightly warmer than the theoretical temperature of absolute zero. Though the difference was less than three degrees on the Kelvin scale, astronomers believe that this heat energy is left from the original big bang. Furthermore, there is as yet no sign of any of the receding galaxies slowing down, which casts doubt on the possibility of the oscillating universe.

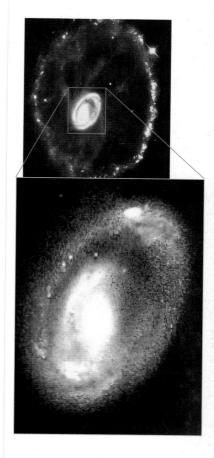

Above Detail of a cartwheel galaxy including a close-up image of the nucleus with comet-like knots of gas.

Left Clusters of infant stars formed in a ring around the core of the barred-spiral galaxy NGC 4314; a close-up reveals dust lanes, smaller bars of stars, and an extra pair of spiral arms packed with young stars.

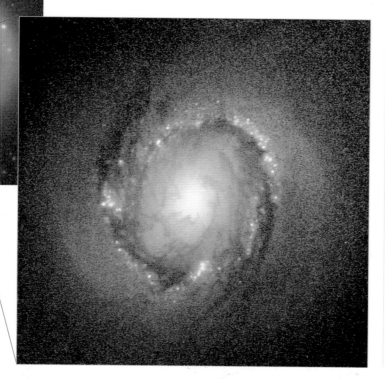

CONSTELLATIONS AND GALAXIES

THIS PAGE AND OPPOSITE PAGE
An image of the grand design of the spiral galaxy M100 resolves individual stars within the majestic spiral arms.

Once radio emissions from hydrogen gas in the Milky Way had shown it was a spiral galaxy, with a series of arms radiating from the center, it became possible to fix the positions of some of our nearest neighbors. For example, stars within the constellations of Orion and Cygnus are located on the same arm of the Galaxy as the Sun. Stars in the constellation of Perseus are located on a different arm, and those of Sagittarius on yet another arm.

The entire galaxy is spinning about its center, with each revolution taking approximately 225 million years. The oldest stars, found at the center of the Galaxy, are some 13,000 million years old. As the Galaxy's rotation accelerated over this time, its motion caused it to flatten out into a spiral disc. Each arm contained huge amounts of dust and interstellar gas, and as these shrank under gravity, they eventually coalesced to form younger stars, like the Sun. More than half the galaxies identified so far are spirals in shape, like the Milky Way, with a dense core of old stars and a thin outer rim, with newer stars lying along a series of outflung arms. Another quarter are barred spirals, rotating more quickly, with a broad band of stars at the center, ending in a curved arm at either end. Most of the remainder are elliptical galaxies, rotating more slowly, and made of mainly older stars.

Galaxies vary widely in size and the number of stars they contain. Spiral galaxies vary between 1,000 million stars and a thousand times this number, and range in breadth from around 20,000 light years to several hundred thousand light years. Elliptical galaxies can measure several million light years across, and contain as many as 10 million million stars. Distances vary from the two million light years separating Earth from the Andromeda galaxy to the 8,000 million light years of the furthest visible galaxy, code named 3C123.

The largest stars of all do not die quietly. Their higher gravity increases the temperature of the central core to prodigious levels, so carbon is consumed to produce a succession of different elements, and finally iron atoms, at its core. By this time, the internal reactions are consuming more energy than they produce. The star collapses and then explodes as a supernova, increasing its brightness up to a billion times, and hurling more than half its matter out into space, producing a nebula that will eventually help to form new stars and planets. The most recent known supernova was seen on February 23, 1987, in the Large Magellanic Cloud, a neighboring galaxy to the Milky Way.

Left behind is the dense central core, shrinking from the blast of the explosion and its own internal gravity. So fierce are these compressive forces, that atoms are crushed into neutrons and a star once larger than the Sun will collapse into a neutron star only a few miles across, and so dense that a spoonful of its matter would weigh hundreds of millions of tons.

Though these neutron stars were predicted as long ago as the 1930s, they were not located until 1967, when radio astronomers observed a series of rapidly pulsing radio sources, which they called "pulsars." These pulses were so regular and so rapid they could only be emitted from a small and fast-spinning object. Since the only bodies in the universe known to be small enough were neutron stars, it was almost certain that these were the mysterious pulsars.

OPPOSITE PAGE
Hot blue stars at the core of M15 that have been stripped of their outer envelope of gas.

THIS PAGE
Top and above A quasar caught in the act of merging or colliding with its companion galaxy. This quasar is so bright that it created diffraction spikes on these telescope images.
Right Three rings of glowing gas encircling the site of supernova 1987A.

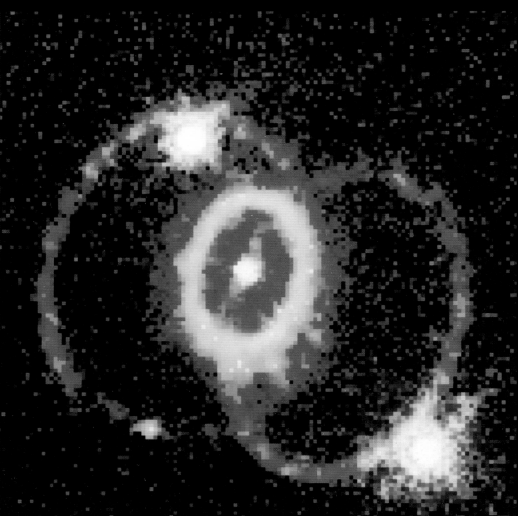

Brilliant objects called quasars, from quasi-stellar radio sources, appear like bright stars when photographed through optical telescopes, but also send out intense radio signals. Consequently, they can be detected over thousands of millions of light years, and are now being seen as they were when the universe was young. Perhaps they are new galaxies in the process of formation, or an early stage in the formation of the universe itself.

At the opposite extreme of visibility lie the equally mysterious black holes. In the very largest dying stars, the forces of internal gravity would be so enormous that they would shrink to a structure even smaller and denser than a neutron star, so that not even light or radio waves could escape, and there would be nothing to reveal their presence.

It is possible that black holes swallow everything that comes within their influence, or that they might even provide a pathway to other universes. So far the only way to identify a black hole is to study the behavior of a visible star orbiting around one, when stellar gas is heated up to emit X-rays as it is compressed under the influence of the black hole's gravity. Special satellites searching for such radiation revealed one massive but invisible object in the constellation Cygnus, which was the first black hole to be identified.

Astronomers have since identified hundreds more stars where these conditions exist, including two stars, Beta Lyrae and Epsilon Aurigae, which are periodically eclipsed by dark discs may well be black holes. Other probable sites for these terrifying and enigmatic stars include the cores of quasars and the center of numerous galaxies, including our own Milky Way. Fortunately, our Sun and solar system are much too far out from the center ever to be affected by the pull of its monumental gravity.

CLASSICS Illustrated

Featuring Stories by the World's Greatest Authors

No. 124   15¢

THE WAR OF THE WORLDS

By H. G. WELLS

HERE BE ALIENS

The human race may not be alone in space, but what are the chances of its meeting with its neighbors? Science fact or science fiction?

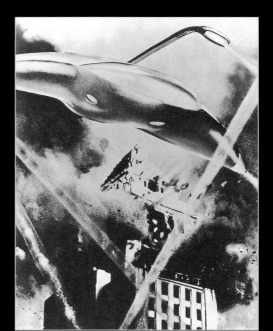

Above Jules Verne (1829–1905), French author of science fiction novels.
Below UFO photographed by Paul Trent at McMinnville, Oregon, U.S. on May 11, 1950.
Below center UFOs over Italy, September 26, 1960.
Below right On July 29, 1952 this UFO was photographed by George J. Stock at Passaic, New Jersey, U.S.

Ever since humans first studied the stars and planets, the possibilities of their harboring other intelligent forms of life have obsessed writers and, more recently, filmmakers. The twin themes of travel to other planets and encounters with visitors from other planets, or star systems, have tended to grow in parallel from surprisingly early beginnings.

In one sense, Lucian of Samosata wrote the first story of travel to the Moon in the second century AD. An explorer attempting to cross the Atlantic was overwhelmed by a great storm which left him shipwrecked on the Moon. By the sixteenth and seventeenth centuries, writers thought the right way to reach Earth's nearest planetary neighbor was to harness birds to a flying chariot. In contrast, Cyrano de Bergerac's *Voyage to the Moon*, of 1656, was positively prophetic, describing the use of multistage rockets to steer the craft to its destination.

However, the first science fiction classic used a less scientifically plausible method to take a craft from Earth to the Moon. Jules Verne, in his 1865 book, *From Earth to the Moon* used a giant cannon to fire his space travelers across the gulf of space. The English writer H. G. Wells in *The First Men on the Moon*, published 36 years later, suggested the use of a mysterious material called Cavorite (after its fictional inventor), which could neutralize the force of gravity.

However, Wells went further than Verne in one respect: he described the Moon as inhabited by a race he called the Selenites. These were giant and intelligent insects that hid from the extreme temperatures at the Moon's surface by digging tunnels linking their living chambers. They proved hostile enough to imprison the explorers and steal their spacecraft. Finally they escaped, though one was recaptured before the other managed to retrieve the spacecraft and return to Earth.

The idea of intelligent but hostile aliens had already been explored by Wells three years earlier, in his 1898 classic *The War of the Worlds*, which described a Martian invasion of England in terrifying detail. His Martians possessed a powerful technology that was proof against all the defensive weapons of the time. They were implacably hostile, and instead of communication between the inhabitants of neighboring planets, the story described how their irresistible progress was defeated only by their susceptibility to Earthly diseases.

The idea of Mars as a source of intelligent, if hostile, life was highly topical at the time. A French astronomer named E. L. Trouvelot had claimed, in 1884, to have detected regular changes in the contrast between the light and dark areas of the Martian surface that he thought were seasonal changes in vegetation. Even earlier, the Italian astronomer G. V. Schiaparelli had observed the appearance of a

TRAVEL THROUGH DEEP SPACE

Even before interplanetary travel was possible, scientists realized that the best way to make a spacecraft with the endurance to make journeys to the other planets of the solar system, would be to assemble it in Earth orbit. Stanley Kubrick's *2001—A Space Odyssey*, in the late 1960s, used a spacecraft for the journey to Jupiter that was a great deal more plausible scientifically, including the use of a powerful computer to control all navigational functions, and a crew that could take it in turns to pass enormous amounts of time in suspended animation within individual life-support pods. Only in the approach to the surface of Jupiter did the film fall back on special effects, in a closing section that still baffles critics.

Kubrick's masterpiece had one fatal flaw, its impossibly optimistic estimate of the date by which such flights would be possible. The television series *Star Trek* avoided this by inventing a completely different, and totally incomprehensible, calendar. This allowed the designers to create an enormous spacecraft in the *USS Enterprise* that was a virtual world in its own right. In its conscious avoidance of the shape of the traditional rocket, it did at least emphasize that the *Enterprise* was designed for much more long-distance flights into deepest space.

Other problems, such as the colossal distances to other star systems were glossed over by the use of warp drive, which was never completely explained. Dramatic devices, such as teleportation to reach other craft and the surfaces of neighboring planets, avoided many other scientific limitations and "Beam me up, Scotty," became a humorous cliché for the need to escape from an awkward or threatening situation.

One of the limitations of traditional science fiction classics is that readers had to rely on the description the authors gave them. As with Wells's Martians, the drama was heightened by suggestion rather than precise detail. Since then, science fiction epics in visual media, such as film and television, have forced the creation of detailed images of spacecraft and alien life forms. In particular, the early epics of space exploration allow comparisons to be made with the technology that has actually been developed to make space travel possible.

The classic film *Destination Moon*, of the early 1950s, clearly based its spaceship on the then current *V2* rocket. It was a cylinder tapering to a point at the top, with a set of broad tailfins. Rather than saving weight by discarding each stage of the rocket as its fuel was exhausted and using the command module and lunar module combination to visit the lunar surface, the whole rocket made both entire journeys.

Landing on the Moon was achieved by using steering rockets to turn the main spacecraft around, and then using the main engine to slow it down to a smooth landing. Taking off from the Moon would be easier, since its gravity is about one-sixth that of Earth. Once the spaceship returned to Earth gravity, it would need to expend colossal amounts of energy to reduce its speed to achieve a second survivable landing.

Above A character from the film *Star Trek.*

Below A still from the film *Destination Moon,* showing the characters dressed in suits based on those used by Nasa astronauts.

Whether friendly or hostile aliens exist or not, sending manned spacecraft over the kinds of distances needed to make contact remains impossible. A slightly more plausible alternative is to send messages, independent of language, on unmanned deep space probes, to show any lifeforms encountering them something of the people who created them, and sent them on their missions.

This was first done with the *Pioneer 10* and *11* spacecraft, sent in the early 1970s to pass Jupiter, before heading out into the depths of space (see chap. 10). Both carried plaques showing outlines of male and female human figures to scale against a drawing of the craft themselves. They also showed the position of Earth relative to the Sun, itself positioned in space relative to important radio stars. Because these craft will continue to travel through space for possibly millions of years, unless captured by the gravity of some massive star or planet, there is a faint possibility that they may eventually be intercepted by beings able to understand the information they carry.

A much faster way to relay information across space is to send it as powerful radio signals traveling at the speed of light. In 1974, a series of 1,679 pulses was sent from the huge Arecibo radio telescope in Puerto Rico. These pulses could be arranged to assemble a diagram showing a human figure, information on prime numbers, and the basic chemical building blocks of life, the components of DNA, the structure of the solar system, and the radio telescope transmitting the signals.

The messages were beamed out in the direction of a cluster of 300,000 stars in the Hercules constellation. Since these are 24,000 light years away, this underlines the enduring impossibility of interstellar communication. The message will take 24,000 years to arrive, and any reply would be seen on Earth a full 48,000 years from now!

Above A pictogram showing the information coded and sent by radio telescope into outer space. *Left* The Pioneer plaque, attached to the spacecraft's antenna.

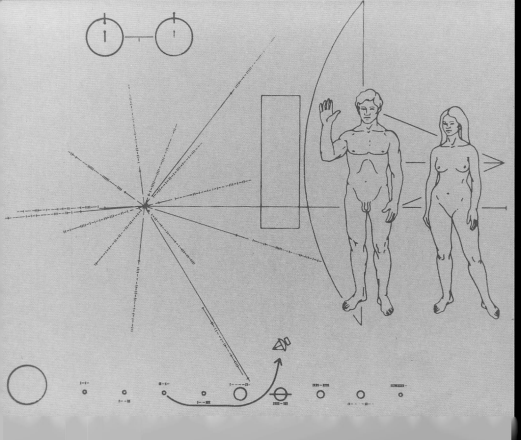

network of thin straight lines, that cross the planet's surface for hundreds, and even in some cases, thousands of miles, which were also subject to these seasonal changes.

The American astronomer Percival Lowell assumed the lines were irrigation canals built by an intelligent race of Martians to channel water from polar ice caps to cities and agricultural areas in the dry equatorial areas. His theories were published at the beginning of the twentieth century, and Wells's scientific background must have made him aware of Lowell's thinking.

While limited to the power of earthbound telescopes, the evidence remained tantalizingly slim, and the possibility of intelligent life on one of our closest planetary neighbors continued to haunt writers of science fiction. Not all agreed with Wells that Martians, if they existed, would pose a hostile threat. Fifty years later, the American writer Ray Bradbury in his *Martian Chronicles* was able to suggest a very different kind of Martian.

Bradbury's stories described how human astronauts visited the red planet to find for themselves the remains of an older, more spiritual civilization, dying out for lack of water on an increasingly arid planet. In Bradbury's stories, the Martians were exploited and corrupted by human colonists that recalled the impact of the Europeans on the Indian tribes of the West, and the roles of heroes and villains were exchanged.

By the time these stories appeared in print, the possibility of genuine aliens had been raised by a series of sightings of mysterious spacecraft. Because of eyewitness descriptions of flat, circular, disc-shaped objects traveling at great height and at impossibly high speeds, they were referred to at first as flying saucers and later as unidentified flying objects or UFOs.

Earlier reports of possible UFOs can be found in accounts ranging back to the Old Testament prophet Ezekiel, but the first modern sightings began in America, with a chain of saucer-shaped objects seen over Washington in 1947 (see p. 36). Within a year the number of claimed sightings had grown so spectacularly that the United States Air Force began to keep a file of these reports in what became known as the Blue Book.

For some reason incidents peaked in 1952, when a series of radar contacts coincided with sightings in the area around the National Airport at Washington D.C., and as a result the U.S. Government instructed the Central Intelligence Agency (CIA) to set up a secret panel of meteorologists, engineers, physicists, and an astronomer, chaired by H. P. Robertson, a physicist from the California Institute of Technology. The panel produced a report indicating that nine out of ten UFO sightings could be explained by natural causes like planets, meteor showers, flocks of birds, clouds of ionized gas, or the northern or southern lights, or by familiar objects like aircraft, searchlights, or balloons.

However, the sightings continued, and another panel was set up in 1966, to reach a similar conclusion. Nevertheless, both reports left open the possibility that a relatively small minority of sightings could not be positively explained by logical causes. In response to this continuing uncertainty, the U.S. Air Force sponsored another study, under the direction of physicist E. U. Condon at the University of Colorado. The resulting report, "A Scientific Study of UFOs," covered fifty-nine UFO sightings in great detail, with contributions from thirty-seven scientists. It firmly rejected the possibility that any of these sightings could be extraterrestrial spacecraft, and recommended that no further investigation should be made. The Blue Book file, containing details of 12,618 sightings in seventeen years, was finally closed.

Not all scientists agreed with the earlier reports. Several experts, including a university astronomer, concluded that a small proportion of the most reliable reports showed definite possibilities of extraterrestrial visitors, and a group of like-minded scientists set up the Center for UFO Studies in Northfield, Illinois, in 1973, to continue research into further sightings.

THEM

Just as with spacecraft, science fiction filmmakers had to produce genuine aliens, rather than eyewitness descriptions. In the simplest cases, with the lowest budgets, these aliens either imitated humans, or took them over and bent them to their wishes, so they could be played by actors with a minimum of makeup. In more ambitious treatments like the notorious Daleks of the BBC television series *Doctor Who*, they were often repulsive or semi-mechanical creatures whose proportions allowed them to accommodate a human actor within the outer casing.

More recently, the Steven Spielberg epic *Close Encounters of the Third Kind*, returned to the flying saucer shape for the alien spacecraft, and the visual equivalent of Wells's vagueness over the physical details of the aliens. However, in Spielberg's *ET*, the extraterrestrial became the hero of the film, and was seen very clearly, so that similarities and differences created a plausible variant on the human species that could indeed have originated on a different planet.

With the honorable exceptions of stories like *ET* and some episodes of *Star Trek*, most fictional aliens have been hostile and threatening. Perhaps the peaks of this science fiction horror combination appeared in the *Alien* series of films, where spectacular special effects created a totally hostile lifeform that could explode from an infected astronaut's chest cavity, and then overwhelm the rest of the crew. These powerful stories sustained several horror films, the ultimate in the enduring view of aliens as enemies.

Below Science fiction comics from the United States and the United Kingdom, which continue to fuel the popularity for this subject.

Ultimately the evidence remains inconclusive. In many cases, the sighting reports show certain common factors. These factors include the suggestion that the UFO is under deliberate and intelligent control, and in cases where more than one is seen, they often seem to be carrying out close-formation flying. In other cases, they seem to make sudden and drastic changes of course, apparently covering enormous distances at prodigious speeds.

On the other hand, optical illusions can deceive the most reliable of observers. Reflections in glass panes or eyeglasses can produce ghostly images, while stationary objects, such as distant planets, can appear to move when seen without a closer visual reference. Even radar traces can result from rain, meteor trails, electronic interference, and reflections from regions of ionization or high humidity.

Those reports describing the appearance of aliens from within the craft often seem to be a result of dreams or hallucinations. Significantly, in nearly all cases they are reported by people who were on their own at the time. Logical explanations would suggest that if these reports were genuine, involving scores of sightings over more than fifty years, occasions where a craft and its occupants were seen by large groups of people or captured on film would have been recorded quite frequently.

Furthermore, the main argument against the extraterrestrial origin for UFOs is one involving physics. As present day astronomers are able to see further and further into the universe, it becomes increasingly likely that there are huge numbers of planetary systems similar to the solar system orbiting nearby stars. By inference, the number of planets capable of supporting intelligent life is relatively high, and such that races of extraterrestrials who have evolved over longer periods to develop technologies infinitely superior to our own, and capable of space travel, are also perfectly possible.

Nevertheless, the possibility of those alien spacecraft crossing the gulfs of interstellar space to reach Earth on a series of reconnaissance missions is virtually non-existent. The best information available to physicists suggests that Einstein's theories of relativity put an absolute limit on the kinds of speeds attainable by any potential spacecraft. Indeed, any craft even moving at a substantial fraction of the speed of light would undergo all kinds of bizarre effects.

Even if it *were* able to reach the speed of light, its mass would become infinite, and it would still take years to reach Earth from the nearest potential planetary system, and years to return. In order to extend the journey to the distances needed for intelligent life to be statistically possible, the journey duration would extend to several lifetimes. Unless another theory eventually undermines Einstein's findings, while the human race may not be alone in space, the chances of its meeting its neighbors are slim indeed.

Below A creature from *Le Voyage Dans La Lune.*

HAVE WE MET BEFORE?

Above Cover of *Fate* magazine, 1948, featuring UFOs.
Below right UFO contactee George Adamski (left) being interviewed on American television by Long John Nebel.

UFO sightings have been regular occurrences since the late 1940s, and even now some of the carefully recorded encounters seem to defy any clear and rational explanation. The original report was filed by businessman Kenneth Arnold, who was flying his own aircraft from Chehalis to Yakima in Washington State on June 24, 1947, when he detoured over the Mount Rainier area to look for the wreckage of a U.S. Marine Corps C-46 transport plane that had been reported missing. To his unbounded surprise, while flying at 9,000 feet (2,740 meters), he spotted a group of nine saucer-shaped craft flying in line-ahead formation some 25 miles (40 kilometers) away, and approximately 500 feet (150 meters) higher. When he timed their passage between Mount Rainier and another nearby peak, he was surprised to find their speed was around 1,700 miles an hour (8,000 kilometers an hour).

The usual explanation, that sightings such as these are caused by optical illusions, could not apply to another sighting of a group of UFOs made on the night of December 6, 1952 by the crew of a U.S. Air Force B-29 bomber over the Gulf of Mexico. There the objects were picked up on the bomber's radar screen, where measurements showed their speed to be more than 5,000 miles an hour (8,000 kilometers an hour). As two of the crew studied the radar, they called out to two other crew members, who peered out into the darkness, to see objects bathed in blue-white light streaking past the bomber at very high speed. Later they were observed, by eye and by radar, returning to the bomber and keeping pace with it, before accelerating away at a speed of some 9,000 miles an hour (14,480 kilometers an hour) before disappearing out of radar range.

In other cases, signs of UFOs landing and taking off were upstaged by incidents where UFOs were said to have exploded or crashed. These, like the classic case of the wreckage found scattered over a ranch near Roswell in New Mexico on July 2, 1947, were usually reported to the authorities, who invariably

picked up the pieces and stored them away far from public view. In view of later statements that no UFO incidents remained unsolved, it seems likely that the wreckage and the explosions had a more mundane explanation, such as crashes involving military aircraft, but this had been obscured in the UFO scares that were prevalent at the time.

Undeniably, the most spectacular claims were made by those who insisted that they had not only seen UFOs landing but had actually met the crews and gone aboard the alien ships. The best known of these was the American George Adamski, who claimed to have encountered an alien from a UFO on November 20, 1952, in the first of a whole series of meetings. Later, he claimed to have been taken aboard a flying saucer from the planet Venus, and then aboard both a "scout" and a "mother ship" from the planet Saturn. As there were no other witnesses, these remained doubtful at best, though Adamski, who died in April 1965, wrote two books based on his experiences.

Others who underwent these close encounter experiences included Betty and Barney Hill, who had been driving home from a holiday in Canada to their home in Portsmouth, New Hampshire on the night of September 19, 1961. They noticed a light moving in the sky, and when their route led them through the passes in the White Mountain range they saw an enormous UFO hovering above the road. They pulled up at a picnic site and Barney examined the craft through binoculars, which clearly showed its occupants peering out of its windows. They rushed back to the car, and then drove off at high speed, fighting an overwhelming sense of drowsiness.

When they overcame this lassitude they found that they had covered thirty-five miles (fifty-six kilometers), from the picnic site, and that two hours had passed. The intervening time was a complete blank, and only later, when they agreed to undergo hypnosis, were they able to recall being taken aboard the spacecraft, separated, subjected to detailed medical examinations, before being released and taken back to their car. The Hills found the experience deeply distressing, and avoided all publicity.

Perhaps most dramatic of all was the case of a young Brazilian peasant farmer named Antonio Villas Boas, who claimed to have been kidnapped on the night of October 15, 1957 by the crew of a UFO who seemed largely human in appearance, and who had taken him aboard their craft. There, he too had been medically examined, including the taking of a blood sample, though he said he had also been persuaded to have sex with a female member of the crew. After more than four hours aboard the ship, he was released and it took off into the night. The farmer was later examined by a doctor who found scars on the skin where Villas Boas had claimed that they had taken the blood sample, but there was no other witness to corroborate the detailed and consistent description he gave of the ship, its occupants and all that had happened to him.

Below Betty and Barney Hill with a sketch diagram of the UFO that apparently abducted them.

THE RISE OF
THE ROCKET

The development of the vehicle that made
space travel possible for the first time.

For all the creativity and imagination of the science-fiction writers, there was only one vehicle that could deliver the power and speed necessary to evade the all-embracing force of gravity. Only the rocket could produce enough thrust, outside the atmosphere, to carry a payload into a stable orbit around Earth, or to journey further toward the other planets of the solar system. Yet a great deal of careful and painstaking work had to be done to move space travel from the pages of fiction and into the real world.

The rocket had been invented by the Chinese, and the principles had been used by the invading Mongols to help them capture Baghdad as long ago as 1258. This knowledge passed to the Arabs, and from them to the Italians, and then the French during the late Middle Ages. British troops were attacked by rockets at the battles of Seringapatam in India

in the last decade of the eighteenth century, and Sir William Congreve developed a series of military rockets for the British Army in the Napoleonic Wars.

Congreve's rockets ranged in eight different sizes, up to a maximum weight of sixty pounds of either high explosive or incendiary material, and were launched from folding ladders. A massed rocket attack against Copenhagen, in 1807, burned down most of the city. Seven years later, during the war between Britain and the United States, a rocket bombardment at the battle of Bladensburg on August 24, 1814 resulted in American forces being outflanked and losing Washington. A month later, the British use of rockets in an attack on Fort McHenry guarding the approaches to Baltimore harbor were immortalized in the line "The rockets' red glare" in "The Star-Spangled Banner."

Unfortunately for the prospects of space travel, all these military rockets burned solid fuel, while being easy to handle and safe to store for long periods, had two supreme disadvantages. Solid fuel was heavy for the amount of thrust it produced, and it was impossible to control. Once the fuel ignited, it burned until it was consumed, and there was no way in which the thrust could be reduced or interrupted to steer a rocket-propelled craft, or to allow it to be landed safely at the end of each flight.

Turning a weapon of war into a sophisticated spacecraft ultimately proved to be a long, complicated, and often disheartening process. It began with a Russian visionary named Konstantin Tsiolkovski, a former provincial schoolmaster and spare-time researcher, who built the first wind tunnel in Russia to investigate aerodynamics and streamlining as part of his quest to design an all-metal airship.

Tsiolkovski was the first to realize the potential advantages of a rocket operating beyond the atmosphere. Because a burning rocket ejects a jet of hot gas backward, it obeys Newton's third law of motion, in producing an

Below A replica of the Congreve bombarding frame of 1806.

equal and opposite reaction to drive it forward. It therefore has no need for an atmosphere that the gases could impact against to create thrust, as is the case with the jet engine, for example. Tsiolkovski realized that this mechanism would work perfectly well in a vacuum, and so the rocket was essential if space travel were ever to become a practical possibility.

Working purely from theoretical knowledge, Tsiolkovski proposed, as early as 1903, that liquid-fueled multistage rockets would be needed to fly from Earth to the neighboring planets. Liquid fuel was essential for the controlling of the thrust, and by dividing the rocket into a series of stages that could be dropped off in flight, as the fuel contained by each stage was exhausted, weight could be reduced to a minimum.

His vision was astonishingly farsighted. His papers appeared while the automobile was still temperamental and inefficient, and the Wright Brothers were still working on their first fragile flying machine. He died in 1935 at the age of seventy-eight, with his ideas still unrealized, by which time the torch had passed to an American named Robert Hutchings Goddard, who also began working on liquid-fuel rockets to make space travel possible.

In Goddard's case, his enthusiasm for the possibility of rocket-propelled space travel began when he read a serialization of H. G. Wells's science fiction classic *The War of the Worlds*, as a teenager in 1898. During the following year he climbed to the top of a cherry tree, in the garden of his family's home in Worcester, Massachusetts, and was so intoxicated with the view that, in the words of his diary, he "...imagined how wonderful it would be to make some device which even had the *possibility* of ascending to Mars... " He climbed down so full of a new sense of belief in what would become his life's work, that, on every October 19 afterward, he celebrated what he called his "Anniversary Day."

Goddard proved Tsiolkovski's theoretical prediction, that a rocket could deliver power in a vacuum, and determined the power output for a range of different fuels, including both liquid oxygen and liquid nitrogen. By the 1920s he was using a rocket motor burning a mixture of gasoline and liquid oxygen, and in a static laboratory test in 1925, Goddard's liquid-fueled rocket succeeded in lifting its own weight. In March of the following year, it flew for the first time, from a field on the farm belonging to his Aunt Effie at Auburn in Massachusetts.

From 1930, Goddard's work attracted enough backing to set up a workshop and test facility at Roswell in New Mexico, where weather conditions were better. By 1935, his liquid-fueled rockets were exceeding the speed of sound and reaching more than a mile above Earth. He had already produced designs and patents for fuel pumps, cooling systems and multi stage rockets, but his work was

Bottom left Goddard standing beside his first liquid fuel rocket on May 16, 1926.
Below A sectional diagram of Goddard's rocket.

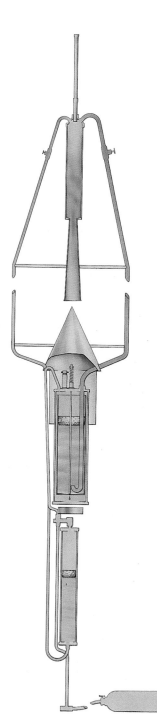

interrupted by the outbreak of war. Because the American Government had no official interest in rocket development, he worked instead on a booster for accelerating seaplanes to take-off speed.

Four days before the Japanese surrender in 1945, Goddard died of cancer of the throat, his life's ambition still unfulfilled. Ironically, during the final years of his life, many of the principles he established were already being put to practical use in weapons development in Germany. It was in Germany that the third of the great rocket pioneers had been working on closely similar lines, but ultimately with much more productive results.

These results were the work of Hermann Oberth who, like Goddard, had read science fiction as a young man. In his case, it had been Jules Verne who had stimulated his interest in space flight, but he too was soon aware that only the rocket offered serious possibilities of traveling beyond Earth's atmosphere. During military service in the Austrian army in World War I, he designed a long-range, liquid-fueled rocket, and the commanding officer of his unit

forwarded it to the Imperial War Ministry. They rejected it as impractical, but after the war Oberth developed his work for a doctorate at Heidelberg University, Germany, in 1922.

Once again his work was rejected, but he published it in book form a year later, showing how rockets could propel a spacecraft to a speed where it would escape from Earth's gravity. He also produced suggestions for electric propulsion, and for spacecraft powered by streams of charged particles as alternatives to rockets, but his mainstream work resulted in the flight of his first liquid-fueled rocket from a launch site near Berlin, Germany, on May 7, 1931.

In 1938, Oberth joined the staff of the Technical University in Vienna, Austria, but during that same year Austria was annexed and incorporated into the Greater German Reich. Oberth himself became a German citizen in 1940, and a year later became a member of the team of scientists working under the direction of Wernhner von Braun at Peenemunde, on the Baltic coast of north eastern Germany, to develop ballistic rockets.

It was in Peenemunde the program began that was to produce not only the wartime V2 rocket that was fired against both Antwerp, Belgium, and London, England, but also the basis for the postwar U.S. space program, which would eventually put men on the surface of the Moon. The beginnings were modest enough, with the liquid-fueled *A* (for Aggregat) *1* of the early 1930s that developed 660 pounds (300 kilograms) of thrust. Pressure from a tank of liquid nitrogen was used to force alcohol and liquid oxygen into the combustion chamber, and the first static tests were successful.

Unfortunately, the extremely volatile fuel mixture meant the slightest shock or spark would cause it to explode violently. The rocket was also very difficult to control when it did work properly. A gyroscope was fitted in the nose and movable control surfaces to the fins of the rocket, but these had little or no influence when the rocket was accelerating at the start of a flight.

Below Wernher von Braun who worked on the V2 rocket.

By early 1935, the much more successful *A2* was ready for its first test flights. This had a revised layout for the control system, and the first two rockets produced were launched from a site on the island of Borkum, off the estuary of the river Elbe on the Baltic coast in Germany. They reached heights of more than 6,000 feet (1,830 meters), and this undoubted success attracted more official interest and financial backing for the whole rocket project.

The *A3* was a much more ambitious design altogether, compared with the two earlier rockets. Its engine burned a mixture of liquid oxygen and alcohol, just like the *A1*, but it developed no less than 3,000 pounds (1,360 kilograms) of thrust. The rocket itself, weighing three-quarters of a ton and standing at more than 20 feet (6 meters), was the largest yet designed.

Unfortunately, the control problem was even more marked with this bigger and heavier rocket. With aerodynamic control surfaces, no matter how sophisticated the control system, there was no way they could steer the rocket during the critical first few seconds of flight,

when it was lifting off from the firing platform. While the rocket was supported on its own fiery exhaust, the slightest instability would cause it to topple over before it could gain sufficient speed.

So severe was the problem of launching an inherently unstable missile, that the *A3* never made a successful flight. By then the attention of von Braun's team had turned to its even more ambitious successor, the *A4*. This was to carry a one-ton payload more than 150 miles (290 kilometers), and the rocket weighed more than 12 tons, and stood at more than 46 feet (14 meters). To produce the planned performance the rocket motor, burning the same volatile fuel mixture of liquid oxygen and alcohol, would have to develop 60,000 pounds (27,200 kilograms) of thrust, and clearly the control problem was now even more urgent.

To solve it, von Braun and his team built a smaller scale model, the *A5*, similar in size to the unsuccessful *A3*, but with a framework using the same techniques as the light, but strong, frames of the giant Zeppelin airships.

Below The *A4* rocket, dubbed by the Nazi propaganda machine the "Vengeance Weapon 2" or "V2."

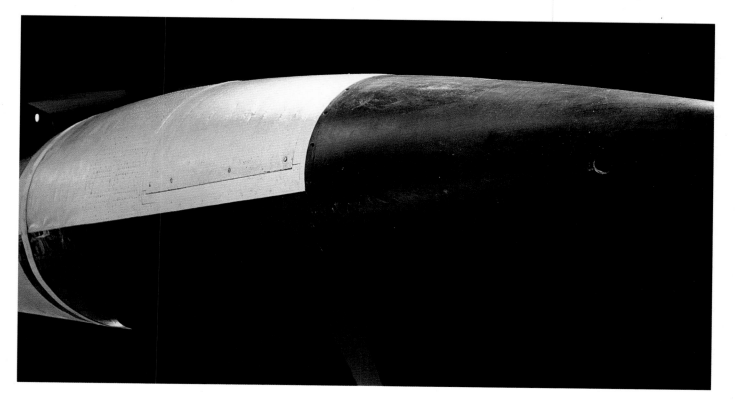

The control system was revised, so the missile could be steered in the critical first few seconds of flight by movable vanes situated in the rocket exhaust. A series of *A5s* was turned out and the rockets were flight-tested over the Baltic during the last year, up to the outbreak of World War II. These tests saw the rockets consistently reaching heights of 35,000 feet (10,670 meters).

Nevertheless, producing the first complete *A4* took another three years of intensive development work. By the time it was ready for firing, on June 13, 1942, it had acquired a new purpose, and a new name. It was now very definitely a weapon, aimed to unleash its cargo of almost a ton of high explosives on cities like Paris and London. Its first official designation, the V2, stood originally for *Versuchsmuster 2*, or *Experimental Type 2*. For propaganda purposes, this was changed to *Vergeltungswaffe 2*, or *Revenge Weapon 2*.

Turning the experimental rocket into a reliable weapon of war was much more difficult than renaming it. Its first flight ended when the fuel pump in the rocket motor failed after a few seconds of acceleration, and the rocket toppled over and exploded. Just over two months later on August 16, 1942, the second V2 was launched. Again the motor failed, though this time the missile accelerated past the speed of sound before slowing and crashing back to Earth. Only on October 3, with the launch of the third V2, did the rocket perform as designed. The missile reached an altitude of 50 miles (80 kilometers) and finally fell to the ground after a flight of almost 120 miles (193 kilometers).

By the time the V2 was ready for mass production, engineering improvements had boosted its range to 260 miles (418 kilometers), with almost three-quarters of its weight taken up by fuel. It accelerated to a maximum speed of more than 3,300 miles per hour (5,310 kilometers per hour), and because it flew far faster than sound, the devastating explosion of its one ton warhead on impact came with absolutely no warning at all. The sound of its flight was only heard by those who survived the blast, and there was no defense against this frightening new weapon.

By September 1944, the first of 4,000 missiles to be launched against Allied targets had been fired at Paris and London. The only limitations on the V2 program were the rate at which the missiles could be produced, the scarcity of the exotic fuels needed to drive them, in a Germany increasingly suffering from Allied bombing and blockade, and the retreat of the German army, which eventually placed potential launching sites out of reach of their intended targets.

By the time the war came to an end, the Allies were all too well aware that German rocket development would be a trump card in postwar competition. Peenemunde and the research establishment lay in what would become the Soviet zone of occupation, together with the Mittelwerke underground factory in the Harz mountains that produced the rockets. The drawings and technical documents from the whole project were buried in an unused salt mine in the British zone. Most of the scientists were taken, under SS guard, to an Alpine village in the southwest of Germany, to escape the advancing Allies, in an area about to be overrun by the Americans.

The result was a scramble for the rockets, the scientists, and the documents, whereby each of the former Allies switched to pursuing their own interests. The British test-fired several V2s from a range in their part of Germany, but it was clear that only the Americans and the Russians had the resources and the determination to mount a major rocket-development program. The scientists in American hands, including most of the control and guidance specialists, were offered contracts to work in the United States. Those in Russian hands, including key rocket-propulsion specialists, were simply put under armed guard and taken by train to the Soviet Union, to continue their work for new masters.

So it was that in the first years of the uneasy peace, V2s were fired from new launch

ROCKET-PROPELLED REVENGE

Above A map of The Hague and Dutch coast in the 1940s, used as reference for V2 rockets.

Right V2 damage in Antwerp, Belgium in 1944.

By autumn 1944, World War II was less than a year from its end, and Hitler's Germany was being crushed from both east and west. Only the totally unstoppable V2 offered a secure means of striking back, and on September 6 the first armed V2 was launched against Paris in France. At seven minutes to seven in the evening of September 8, the first V2 aimed at London exploded in suburban Chiswick, on the western side of the city. Sixteen seconds later another impacted in Epping to the north, heralding the start of a six month campaign of terror and destruction.

The completely unpredictable arrival of a V2 was terrifying in the extreme. Each one-ton warhead killed an average of five people. Moreover, because the missile flew faster than sound, the noise of its approach could only be heard after the explosion. An additional factor contributing to its immunity to Allied countermeasures was the use of mobile launchers, which proved virtually impossible to spot.

By early April 1945, when the German armies had finally been pushed back far enough to put Allied cities out of rocket range, more than 4,000 V2s had been launched against Paris, London, and Antwerp. A total of 1,359 V2s were fired at London, of which only 169 were known, to the Germans, to have failed en route. British records showed that 1,115 exploded on British soil, but the accuracy of the rocket was clearly a continuing problem. London was a huge target, but rather less than half the missiles, 501 in all, actually fell within the London Civil Defence Region.

UNRAVELLING THE V2 SECRETS

Though there was little the British could do to stop the V2s from reaching London, they were already aware of the threat. They had inspected parts of a crashed V2s which veered off course from Peenemunde and came down in Sweden on June 13, 1944, less than three months before the attack began. More valuable information came from the Polish Resistance, who had been watching the test firings of V2s from a German range at Blizna in eastern Poland.

Time and again they would rush to a crash site, only to find German patrols had carried off vital components for analysis. Only

Below **The first launch from Cape Canaveral of a V2 rocket.**

on May 20, 1944, when one crashed near a village called Sarnaki, on the banks of the river Bug, were they first on the scene. Lacking the time to move it before the Germans arrived, the Resistance men rolled the wreckage into the river and screened it with a herd of cows to stir up the mud.

The Germans failed to find the rocket, and the Poles were able to dismantle it in peace, and make detailed drawings. The Allies agreed to send an unarmed DC3 transport plane to make a night landing at an unused airfield deep in German-occupied Poland, and pick up the parts and the drawings.

These were carried by a Polish Resistance agent, who cycled 200 miles (320 kilometers) through the retreating German army, with his precious cargo carried in a sack slung over his shoulder. Finally, he and the sack were ready at the landing ground on July 26, when the DC3 was on its way from Brindisi in Italy. Then, to the infinite horror of the Poles hidden alongside the airfield, two German fighters landed on the field. Had they been betrayed, and were the fighters waiting for the RAF plane?

To their unbounded relief, the fighters started up and took off as darkness fell. Just before midnight the DC3 landed, and parts and drawings were loaded on board. But when the pilot tried to take off, the aircraft refused to move, its tires stuck in the mud from recent heavy rain. With the engines running at full power, and their roar echoing across the silent countryside, the whole enterprise seemed doomed.

Only quick action by local farmers saved the day. They tore down nearby fences and laid the planks on the field to take the weight of the aircraft. Helpers scrabbled away at the mud around the wheels with spades and their bare hands, and finally the plane began to move, slowly accelerating to takeoff speed. As it vanished into the night the German forces arrived, running into a resistance ambush. Within three days the parts and drawings were safely in London.

sites on both sides of the world. The pioneering work of the German teams working at Peenemunde would be vital, in Russian hands, in helping to place the first satellite in orbit around Earth, and putting the first man into space. Progress on the American side would seem slower and more uncertain, but in time the knowledge developed on Germany's Baltic shore would provide the basis for the Saturn rocket, which would propel astronauts to land on the surface of another planet.

When the missiles that were the fruits of the Peenemunde program finally arrived in Russia and America, much work still lay ahead for both sides. The Americans had seized 100 assembled V2s, ignoring British protests that wartime agreements entitled them to half the missiles, and moved the missiles and their team of German scientists to the White Sands Proving Ground in New Mexico.

The first American V2 passed a static test on March 14, 1946. A second rocket was fitted with a payload of instruments, and launched to a height of 67 miles (108 kilometers) on June 28, 1946. Following a long series of test launches all went well until

May 29, 1947, when a V2 veered across the border into Mexican airspace. It crashed into a cemetery in Juarez, fortunately missing the crowds at a local fiesta. In spite of this mishap, the rest of the program continued successfully.

The first Russian V2 was launched from a site in the steppes of Kazakhstan on the morning of October 30, 1947, after a delay of an hour caused by the partial collapse of the firing platform. It flew for 185 miles (298 kilometers), and crashed back to earth precisely on target. The missile race and the space race had begun. Both started promisingly for the Americans, with the launching of a V2-boosted WAC Corporal rocket on February 28, 1949 to a record altitude of 259 miles (417 kilometers), an achievement not beaten for another eight years.

Nevertheless, their Soviet opposite numbers would deliver a series of profound shocks during the next decade. However, the ultimate triumph would lie with the U.S. team and their German colleagues, with the development of the multistage Saturn liquid-fueled rocket, which would carry the Apollo moonflights.

Above **The V2 in the United States, at the Air Force Missile Test Center.**

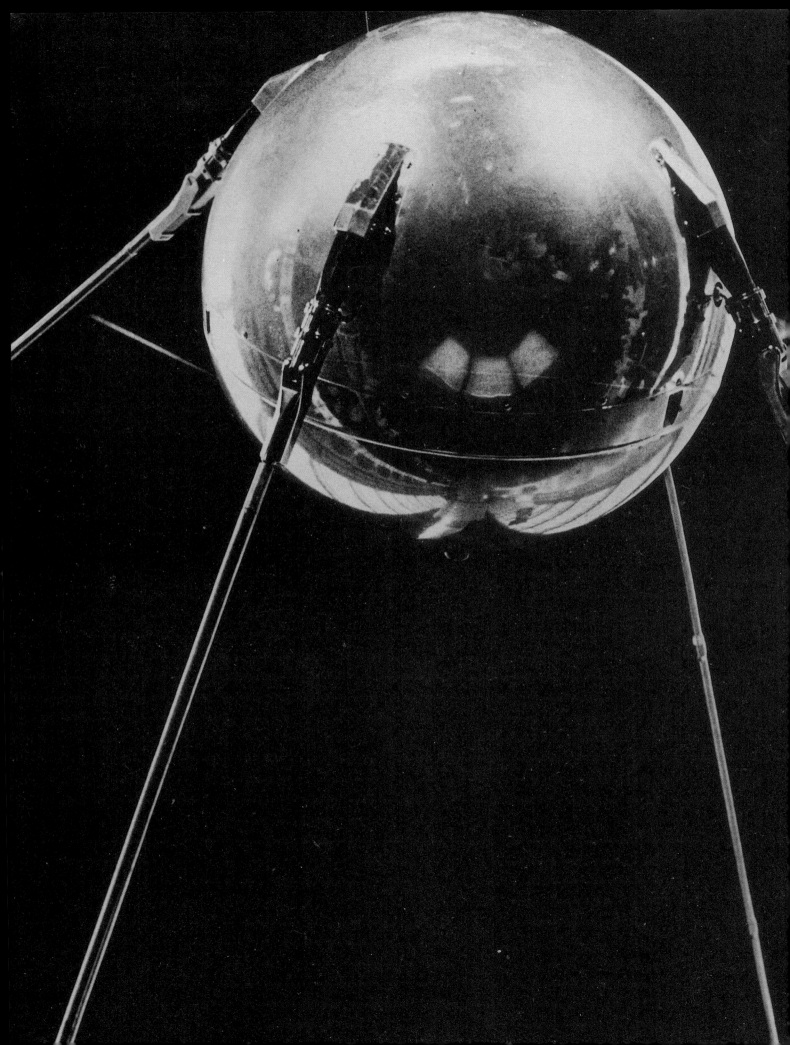

FELLOW TRAVELERS: LAUNCHING THE FIRST SATELLITES

As the Soviet *Sputnik 1* rocketed into orbit, the first satellite in space, the international space race was truly underway.

OPPOSITE AND THIS PAGE
The world's first artificial Earth satellite, launched by the Soviet Union on October 4, 1957.

Whatever dates are selected as representing the dawn of the Space Age, one serious contender must be October 4, 1957. On the evening of that day, a Soviet rocket succeeded in putting the first artificial satellite into orbit around Earth, and in doing so dealt a devastating blow to American hopes of leading the world in space exploration.

The satellite was named *Sputnik* (Russian for "fellow traveler") *1* and was spherical in shape, weighing 184 pounds (83 kilograms). It was placed in an elliptical orbit so that its height above Earth's surface varied from 584 miles (940 kilometers) at its highest point to 143 miles (230 kilometers) at its lowest. The regular bleeping of its battery-powered radio transmitter could be heard all over the world, and provided a constant reminder of this remarkable Russian achievement.

In fact, the Russians had given clear signals of what they intended to do. While the Americans had concentrated on using their initial stock of German-made *V2s* as the stepping stone to developing other rockets of their own design, the Russians had begun their space program by building more powerful versions of the German missiles, which were capable of ranges up to 500 miles (800 kilometers) or more. The Russians concentrated their efforts on missile development, that is, primarily producing rocket engines that would eventually have the performance and endurance to cross the world and threaten the United States, and it took just a decade of hard work to produce a rocket that could carry a two ton warhead more than 4,000 miles (6,930 kilometers). This was achieved by 1957.

Up to this point, the only reason for Russian rocket development had been military. However, the problem with such a spectacular new weapon was persuading potential adversaries that it actually existed. Fortunately, for the Soviet Union's position in the space race, 1957 had been designated the International Geophysical Year, and the country's leader Nikita Sergeyevich Khrushchev

was persuaded that using the new Russian rocket to launch a small, but simple, satellite would have two enormously valuable results. It would show the supremacy of Russian technology, and it would demonstrate that the rocket's performance was genuine, with powerful implications for international negotiations.

In June 1957, Russia announced that a satellite was ready, and in September they announced the wavelength to be used by its radio transmitter. The Americans at first refused to believe that a successful launching would take place. Although they were working on rocket development, progress had been much slower and more deliberate, as all three armed services had begun working on a number of different missiles that would one day be powerful enough to deliver nuclear warheads to the opposite hemisphere. For the time being, the United States was content to base the deterrent force on nuclear weapons carried aboard manned bombers.

So the news of the Russian launch of *Sputnik 1* broke, with all the drama of a bomb being detonated within the corridors of power of the U.S. administration. The Soviet rocket was later revealed to consist of two stages, each one fitted with four rocket engines, together with four strap-on booster pods, each one containing four more rocket engines burning a mixture of kerosene and liquid oxygen. This enormously powerful combination had achieved a speed of 18,000 miles per hour (28,900 kilometers per hour), sufficient to place the satellite into orbit, where it remained, bleeping its message of Russian success to the world for three months before Earth's gravity overcame it and it burned up on reentry into the atmosphere.

President Eisenhower had announced two years before that the Americans would be launching Earth satellites as part of the International Geophysical Year program, and by now it was clear to the whole world they had been beaten to it. Unfortunately, many of their problems were self-inflicted. The German experts under Wernher von Braun were working for the U.S. Army on a powerful and promising rocket called the Redstone. The U.S. Air Force had a missile called the Atlas that had been developed as a potential ballistic missile, and the U.S. Navy had developed a three stage satellite-launching rocket called Vanguard, that was based on a civilian research rocket called the Viking.

Amazingly, the administration chose the least promising of the three projects, the Vanguard. The Air Force was persuaded to join in backing the program, while the Army's Redstone project was written out of the script altogether. As a result, the Vanguard's payload limitations were so severe that the first U.S. satellite weighed just three and a half pounds (1.6 kilograms), less than one-fiftieth of the weight of *Sputnik 1*.

Even before this first hesitant step into the future could be taken, the Russians increased their lead. Just over four weeks after the launch of *Sputnik 1*, they launched *Sputnik 2*, a satellite six times the size of *Sputnik 1*, on November 3, 1957. *Sputnik 2* carried a small dog named Laika, the first living creature to voyage into space, together with a life-support system, instruments to record her temperature, heartbeat, and other vital functions, as a signpost to show whether human beings could survive in space, and a transmitter to relay the data back to Mission Control. The first launch of Vanguard and its tiny satellite was scheduled for more than a month later, on December 6. Unfortunately for American hopes, the launch was a disaster. At six minutes to midday the Vanguard rocket rose off its launching pad, then toppled over on its side and exploded. Yet the first steps to retrieve the situation had already been taken. Von Braun and his team had been developing a multistage version of the Redstone rocket that had been named *Jupiter-C*. This was made by adding an extra booster stage containing a battery of eleven solid-fuel rocket motors, and weighed three times as much as the similarly-sized Vanguard. The first of these rockets had been successfully

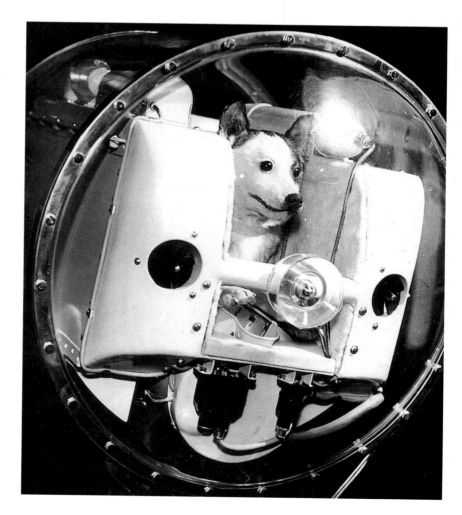

OPPOSITE PAGE
Failure of the U.S. Vanguard launch vehicle on its launch pad on December 6, 1957.

THIS PAGE
Left A jubilant report in an Alabama newspaper in the United States about the successful launch of the *Jupiter-C* missile on January 31, 1958.
Below A model of the dog Laika in the container that was sent up with the second Sputnik on November 3, 1957.

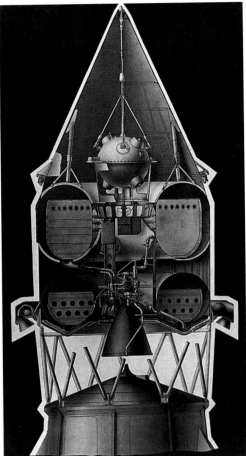

Above *Luna 2* automatic station.
Above right A diagram of the
Luna 1 space station.

launched in 1956, reaching a height of 600 miles (965 kilometers) and a range of 3,000 miles (4,830 kilometers), which was a great deal better than any of its American rivals. Hurriedly the administration reversed its policy, and switched responsibility for launching America's second satellite, the thirty-one pound *Explorer 1*, to the army and *Jupiter-C*.

By January 31, 1958, *Explorer* was ready to launch, and the occasion was a triumph for von Braun and his team. The rocket blasted off without a hitch, and the satellite was safely placed into Earth orbit. Though it was still significantly smaller than the Russian satellites, America had a powerful lead in electronics and instrumentation. Almost immediately it was established in orbit, with *Explorer's* instruments detected electrically charged atoms in such abundance that the recorders went off the

scale. The satellite had encountered what came to be called the van Allen radiation belts, after James van Allen, the scientist responsible for the experiment. These were belts of protons and electrons from the Sun, carried on the solar wind and trapped by Earth's magnetic field.

It took another six weeks for Vanguard to launch its miniature satellite successfully, by which time the Russians were poised for their next lunge forward in the race between the superpowers. On May 15, 1958, *Sputnik 3* rose into orbit, capitalizing to the full on the sheer power of the Russian rockets. Fully two-thirds of the satellite's ton and a half weight was taken up by instrumentation and transmitting facilities. Clearly, it would not be long before the Russians succeeded in putting the first human astronaut on a space voyage.

In the United States it was clear that the Voyager program would never have the power

In early satellite launches, limited power meant it was essential to use every means of assisting the satellite into orbit. For example, Earth's spinning on its axis meant that launching sites near the equator were moving rapidly from west to east relative to the surrounding space. Consequently a rocket that was launched vertically would be traveling eastward as Earth rotated beneath it. If the rocket was then steered to an eastward trajectory, it and the satellite it carried would reach a greater velocity relative to Earth than if it had been launched to the west, and could therefore be established in a higher orbit. This was called hitching a ride, and was used in most of the early satellite launches.

As the equipment for launching satellites became more reliable, and the precision of controls allowed the resulting orbits to be selected with great accuracy, different types of coverage of Earth's surface became possible. Satellites designed to relay communications between different ground transmitters, like TV satellites and military communications satellites, are usually launched on an orbit that parallels the equator. The height of the orbit is chosen so that the satellite's speed through space is matched by the rotation of Earth below it.

This means the satellite effectively hovers over the same spot on the surface in what is called a geosynchronous orbit, even though it is actually moving through space at very high speed. The intention is that the satellite's footprint, or the area covered by its reradiated transmissions, will remain the same in spite of the rotation of Earth.

Satellites monitoring Earth weather systems or collecting intelligence on natural resources or military deployments need to cover the whole of the planet's surface in successive orbits. These are launched in an orbit that takes them over the North and South Poles on each circuit, so that as the planet rotates beneath their path, they will cover its entire surface on successive passes.

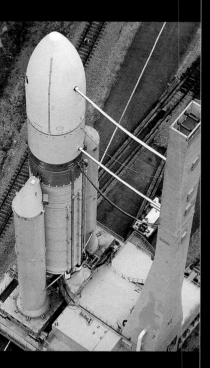

Above The European rocket
Ariane 5 on its launch pad.
Right The launch of Britain's first
satellite, *Ariel 1* in April 1962.

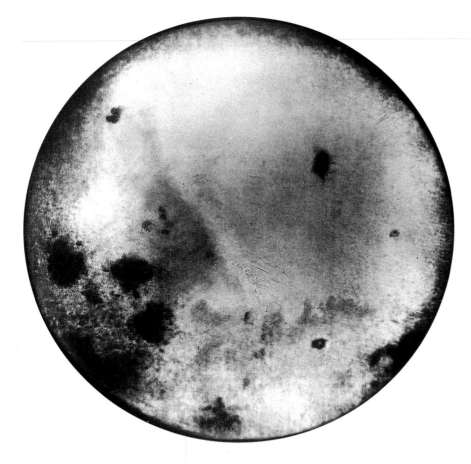

to do this. The only serious contenders both owed their existence to the captured German rocket scientists. In addition to von Braun's *Jupiter* rocket, the U.S. Air Force was developing plans for a reusable hybrid rocket plane called the Dyna Soar, under the direction of von Braun's former boss at Peenemunde, retired Major General Walter Dornberger. Although this would never be carried through to a prototype, the basic principles would eventually be developed into the space shuttle (as described in chap. 8).

Because the U.S. administration, for reasons of its own connected with limiting the influence and expense of big defense-based contracts wanted to maintain a clear separation between military rockets and an essentially civilian space program, President Eisenhower wanted to establish a civilian authority to direct the whole project.

On the recommendation of his scientific advisers, he took the existing National Advisory Council for Aeronautics established in 1915 to coordinate aeronautical research and development. On April 2, 1958, the council was given the new name of the National Aeronautics and Space Agency, under the acronym NASA —though the name was changed later so that the initials stood for the National Aeronautics and Space Administration, to reflect the organization's wider responsibilities.

At first, NASA had two targets. In order to avoid leaving space exploration to the Russians, it was decided to put an American astronaut into space as soon as possible. From the viewpoint of the Moon, it was decided to develop a series of unmanned vehicles to carry out the exploration of the nearest of the planets. Von Braun and his team moved from the U.S. Army program to work directly for NASA, at the misleadingly named Jet Propulsion Laboratory at Pasadena. Meanwhile, the Russians were continuing to forge ahead, even in this new area of space exploration in which the U.S. had just declared an interest.

On January 2, 1959, a Russian rocket launched the spherical satellite *Luna 1*, which flew past the Moon as it became the first object to escape Earth's gravitational field once and for all. After passing beyond the Moon's weaker gravitational influence, transmitting information all the time, it headed out into a permanent orbit around the Sun, to become the first artificial solar satellite. As if that was not enough, *Luna 2* was launched on September 12, 1959, and aimed fairly and squarely at its lunar target. It ended its flight by crashing into the Moon's surface a day later. Pride of place in this early moon-exploration series of launches went to *Luna 3*, launched only three weeks later. This entered an orbit that took it around the far side of the Moon, that had always remained invisible from Earth, and the pictures it sent back to base were the first views of this hitherto unseen aspect of lunar geography.

All of this was making American efforts seem pedestrian by comparison. Nevertheless, their ability to place satellites in Earth orbit was being used to demonstrate their lead in expertise and equipment for sophisticated observation and research applications. In 1960, two radical, new, special-purpose satellites were launched. *Echo 1* was a plastic balloon coated with aluminum that was able to reflect radio signals beamed at it from the surface of Earth and relay them back to Earth at a spot normally inaccessible because of the curvature of Earth's surface.

Second, the television and infrared observation satellite (TIROS) was launched in April 1960, and was the first weather-monitoring satellite. It carried television cameras powered by batteries charged by energy from solar cells. These cameras were trained on Earth's cloud cover to relay data on weather systems and watch the development and growth of storm systems.

By 1961, the picture of the space race had changed completely. The Americans' progress had been so rapid that they very nearly beat the Russians in putting the first human astronaut into space (see chap. 6). Furthermore, the change of president with the election of John F. Kennedy to replace Dwight D. Eisenhower, resulted in an equally radical change in NASA's objectives. From now on the organization's most important objective was not to be the exploration of the Moon with remote, unmanned probes, but the landing of astronauts on the moon before the end of the decade (see chap. 7).

During the 1960s, the Americans modified several ballistic missiles to serve as more powerful launch vehicles. The first was a missile called the *Titan II*, which had two solid-fuel booster rockets strapped to the liquid-fueled missile. The same treatment was applied to the liquid-fueled Thor intermediate-range ballistic missile, and later both Atlas and Titan missiles had an additional liquid oxygen/liquid hydrogen fueled final stage added to boost heavy military satellites into orbit.

During the four decades since the original satellite launches, rocket launchers have become so reliable and so predictable that they have an outstanding safety record. Now the

ingenuity and expertise are concentrated on the orbiters themselves, to wring more information out of Earth and the space environment it inhabits, and on lowering the cost of satellite launching. In spite of the initial lead enjoyed by both America and Russia from their development of ballistic missiles, other nations have now joined the race to place satellites in orbit, either by developing their own launch vehicles or reaching an agreement with countries who have this technology.

France successfully launched a satellite in 1965, followed by Japan and the People's Republic of China in 1970, and the United Kingdom in 1971. More recently, the Western European countries set up the European Space Agency program to develop the Ariane booster rocket, which uses solid fuel in its first two stages, and a cryogenic engine in the third and final stage. This is powerful enough to launch two satellites at once, equivalent to the American delta class, each weighing one and three-quarter tons, or a single satellite weighing up to four and a half tons. These massive weights are comparable to the payload of the space shuttle, and future developments of the rocket are intended to lift still heavier satellites into orbit.

Two projects for future low-cost launchers are currently being developed in the United States. The Lockheed Martin Corporation are working on the Reusable Launch Vehicle concept, which operates on a similar principle to the space shuttle, taking off vertically on rocket motors and landing horizontally like an aircraft. In this case, though, it has no crew aboard, and has no separate boosters to be jettisoned during flight. Meanwhile, a multinational consortium headed by Boeing is converting an offshore oil-drilling platform into a mobile launch pad that could be towed to the equator, where the satellites would be given the maximum benefit from Earth's own rotation, when launched by former Soviet rockets now being marketed at competitive prices by both Russia and the Ukraine.

NEW TYPES OF SATELLITES
AND SATELLITE WARFARE

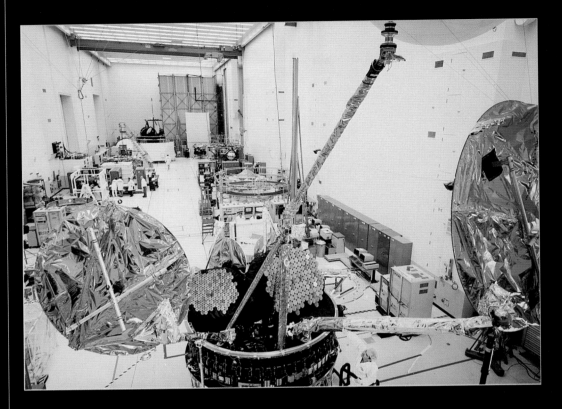

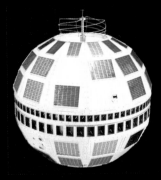

Above The *Telstar 1* satellite, 1962.

Above right Assembly of the *Intelsat VI* satellite.

With improvements in satellite instrumentation, and the development of reliable and cost-effective launchers, more and more specialized types of satellite, have been introduced. For example, the success of the TIROS weather satellite paved the way for satellites that could provide global coverage of the dark side of Earth, and later a network of geosynchronous satellites to provide constant cover of the area of the globe covered by their stationary footprint. In addition to their own instruments, these satellites are able to collect and relay data from remote unmanned ground and ocean-based sensor stations to build up additional information for the overall weather picture.

Satellites have also become vital aids to navigation. Their elevated view of Earth's surface has allowed the relative positions of the world's major landmasses to be plotted more accurately. Apart from satellite-based navigation systems like GPS, which enable ships, aircraft, and even individuals to determine their position with great accuracy

even in the poorest visibility and in the absence of any discernible landmarks, specialized satellites use radar to uncover a mass of information about Earth itself. The Landsat series of satellites have used different types of spectral imaging to monitor agriculture and land use, forestry and mineral deposits, and water supplies.

The U.S. Navy's Geosat satellite uses a special type of imaging radar to map ocean currents and the contours of the seabed. The Laser Geodynamic Satellite (LAGEOS) was launched as long ago as 1976 into a very high orbit some 3,600 miles (5,790 kilometers) above Earth that should give it an operating life of several million years! LAGEOS is a passive satellite with an outer aluminum sphere covered with 426 reflectors that enable ground-based lasers to be used to measure tides, continental drifts, and even slippages along geological fault lines, all of which make earthquake prediction more reliable. Finally, communications satellites now relay telephone

Earth where surface transmissions suffer from variations in ionospheric conditions.

Many specialized types of satellites were developed to give the earliest possible warning of a potential ballistic missile attack. This made them prime targets for any nation contemplating a first strike to maintain the essential element of surprise and prevent an instant response from their adversaries. A series of different methods were developed by the Russians for destroying satellites in low Earth orbit by moving other controllable satellites close enough to them to deliver a killer punch.

Some of these hunter-killer satellites were suicide weapons in that they destroyed the enemy satellite by exploding at close range. Others launched a small cloud of metal pellets or needles into the path of the other satellite, which, given the colossal speeds attained by orbiting objects, would be enough to destroy it entirely, or at the very least cripple and render it useless. However, these methods were limited in their range, since they were essentially massive and cumbersome, which limited them to low orbits, on top of which, their performance was relatively poor. Maneuvering them into an attack position took a long time, and satellites in higher orbits were likely to be out of range.

The Americans retaliated by experimenting with other ways of destroying satellites. They developed a series of missiles that could be launched against satellite targets. The first of these were launched from ground sites, but later the Reagan administration backed the development of a Miniature Homing Vehicle (MHV), a smaller missile that could be launched from a specially equipped F-15 fighter and was accurate enough to score a direct hit on the target and destroy it without the need for explosives. As the F-15 was carried aboard U.S. Navy aircraft carriers, the weapon

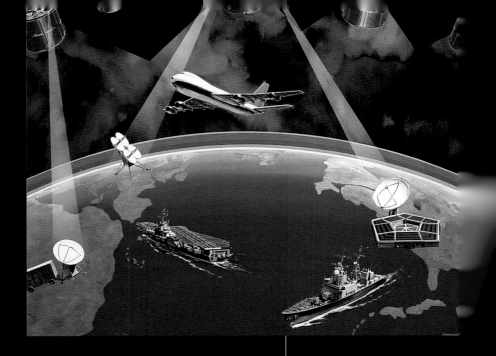

could theoretically be launched from most parts of the globe, but although the fighter could launch the missile at heights of up to 10 miles (16 kilometers), the missile could still only hit satellites in relatively low orbits.

The theme was extended in the Strategic Defense Initiative, popularly known as Star Wars. This was based on a series of antimissile weapons which were themselves satellites in orbit around Earth. They included infrared telescopes to detect missile launches, and laser radars to track their flight, reinforced by high-energy spaceborne lasers to destroy the missiles by burning holes through their outer skin. Whether all this sophisticated technology would actually work in the case of a genuine attack was never proved, since experts estimated that multiple targeting would present the defenses with more than 100,000 ballistic warheads, each of which could have been given a tougher outer skin relatively easily to render it less vulnerable to bursts of laser energy.

Top An artist's impression of the constellations of *Defense Satellite Communications System 2* in geostationary earth orbit in the 1970s.
Above An illustration of the *Intelsat 5* communication satellite, 1980.

MANNED
SPACE FLIGHT

Rapid developments in technology led to longer and more ambitious flights, space walks, and the possibility of one day landing on the moon.

OPPOSITE PAGE

Yuri Gagarin, the first man in space, at the
command desk of the
Vostok rocket, 1961.

THIS PAGE

The dog sent into space on the Soviet
Interplanetary rocket *Space Ark* in August 1960.

Both the Americans and the Russians were racing to be the first to put a human astronaut into space. The initial lead of the Russians with the spectacular launch of *Sputnik 1* in October 1957, described in chap. 5, had been largely eroded by American superiority in electronics, instrumentation, and control, but the Soviet Union had been first by a considerable margin to launch animals into space. The sacrifice of the original space dog Laika, who had made a one-way mission into Earth orbit, was followed by *Sputnik 5*, which launched and recovered two dogs on August 20, 1960. Both dogs survived their trip into space with no apparent ill effects.

By now the Americans were close behind with their Project Mercury, targeted with placing a man aboard a satellite. On January 31, 1961, a spacecraft containing a chimpanzee called Ham was lobbed into space on a trajectory that brought it back into the atmosphere before a full orbit had been completed. The technology seemed to have been proved, and astronaut Alan Shephard was training to complete a similar suborbital flight, which was planned for the middle of March, a mere six weeks later.

There was, however, one problem, which sounded a note of warning. The Redstone booster that had propelled Ham into space had provided rather too much thrust so that the spacecraft was delayed in returning to Earth. Though Ham was unharmed, the decision was taken to carry out further testing to make sure all was well before Shephard was launched into space. The launch was postponed for almost two months for this process to be carried out.

The decision was prudent but disastrous for American prestige. On April 12, 1961, some four weeks after the original date for Shephard's planned flight, a Soviet rocket launched a Vostok spacecraft into orbit carrying Lieutenant Yuri Gagarin. He not only completed a full orbit, but his spacecraft made a faultless reentry into Earth's atmosphere and Gagarin was able to parachute down to a soft landing on the Russian steppe. Once again, the Soviet Union had scored a dramatic first place in yet another heat of the Space Race.

Shephard finally took off on May 5, 1961, just over three weeks after his Russian rival. The American project was still lagging behind Soviet capabilities, as the less powerful U.S. rocket could not lift a large enough payload to allow the *Mercury* capsule to descend over land. Instead, the trajectory was calculated to drop the returning astronaut into the Atlantic, where the capsule was to be picked up by rescue helicopters from a U.S. Navy carrier. Furthermore, Shephard was in space for only 15 minutes, reaching a height of 115 miles (185 kilometers), but it was a sign that the Americans were catching up.

To reinforce the message that this was no mere fluke, a second Mercury suborbital flight was launched on July 21, 1961, when U.S. astronaut Virgil "Gus" Grissom went through the same drill as Shephard. The craft splashed down in the ocean, and this time the explosive bolts securing the hatch went off long before the rescuers had arrived. By the time they were on the scene, Grissom had had to abandon his sinking capsule, and the decision was made to make the hatch more difficult to open, on the grounds of safety.

Then the Russians were off again, with cosmonaut Herman Titov lifting off on August 6, 1961, and spending more than twenty-four hours in space, making a series of seventeen orbits of Earth. Titov himself slept for part of his mission and also ate a series of specially prepared meals, although he complained afterward that the weightless conditions made him feel severe nausea.

By February 20, 1962, with a more powerful rocket at their disposal, the Americans were at last ready for a full orbital flight. This was the *Atlas D*, adapted from the Atlas intercontinental ballistic missile developed for the U.S. Air Force launched the *Friendship* capsule containing astronaut John Glenn into space. His target was three orbits at a height of between 100 miles (161 kilometers) and 163 miles (262

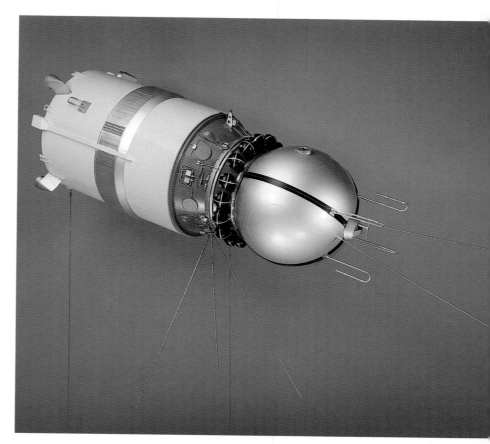

kilometers), which was less than the Russians were currently achieving. Even so, a system malfunction nearly led to disaster, but ultimately demonstrated the superiority of American technology and adaptability.

While the flight was in progress, instruments on the ground at Mission Control revealed that the spacecraft's heat shield had been loosened. Already Glenn had had to deal with a problem involving a control jet defect, but this was potentially far more serious. The heatshield was designed to be burned up, absorbing the friction and heat energy of the reentry into the atmosphere. If it was to break off on reentry the results would be fatal, and the ground control team had to work very quickly indeed for the time when the retro-rocket would need to be fired to slow down the capsule to initiate its descent.

The result was an inspiration. Instead of the normal sequence, which would jettison the retro-rocket when it had been fired, Mission Control ordered Glenn to keep it in place. Because it was mounted in the center of the heatshield, it should provide a measure of protection and also help to hold the assembly in place. Glenn fired it on cue, the rocket assembly remained in place as did the

heatshield, and the *Friendship* capsule splashed down in the sea as intended. When the capsule was examined, the heatshield was found to be in perfect order, as the malfunction had been in the monitoring instruments!

The Russians retaliated with not one flight but two. On August 11, 1962, Andrian Nikolaev went into orbit for a four-day flight, to be followed on August 12 by Pavel Popovich, in an identical craft on a similar mission. There was some speculation that some kind of docking maneuver might have been intended, but this was not carried out, and succeeding Soviet flights, while impressive, tended to create the impression that they were being forced into ever more extravagant gestures to obscure the fact that the Americans were clearly closing the gap between the space powers' efforts.

Both the Americans and the Russians were about to leave behind the initial and limited one-occupant spacecraft missions, with the

OPPOSITE PAGE
Launch of the *Friendship* capsule in 1962.

THIS PAGE
Above left Herman Titov and Adrian Nikolayev on *Vostok 2*, August 6, 1961.
Above A model of the *Vostok 1* capsule, 1961.

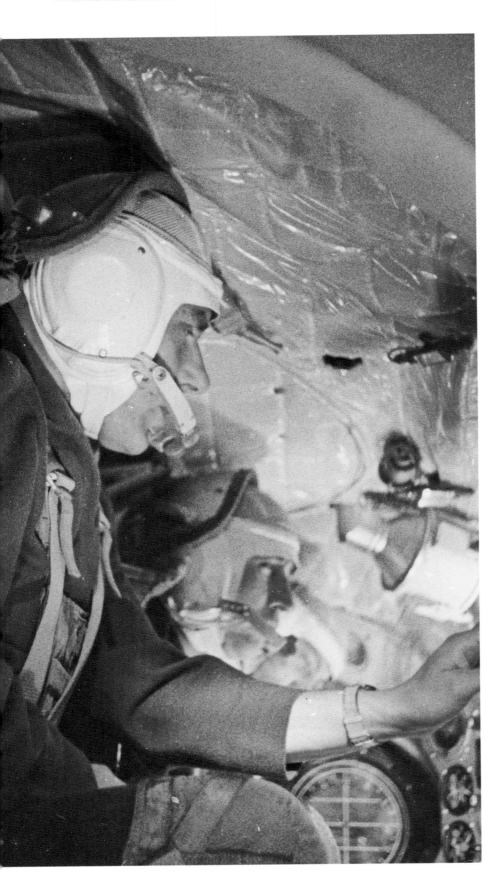

advent of still more powerful launchers. The last two missions in the Mercury program were made for longer flights than before. On October 2, 1962, Walter Schirra spent nine hours in space, but ran into similar problems to those encountered by Titov on the first Russian twenty-four-hour mission. The longer period spent in weightless conditions meant that when he returned to Earth he suffered vertigo and circulatory problems. Finally, on May 15, 1963, Gordon Cooper spent no less than thirty-four hours in space. Though this was still a brief glimpse by Russian standards, he was able to carry out complex controlled maneuvers, steering his spacecraft by directional rocket motors, and he also took a series of photographs of Earth's surface from his elevated viewpoint.

The last two flights in the series of Vostok single-person spacecraft launches were made in June 1963. *Vostok 5* was launched on June 14, carrying Valery Bykovsky, and once again was quickly followed by another Vostok, launched on June 16. This was another "first," though in a completely different respect from other Soviet triumphs, as it was carrying the world's first female space traveler, Valentina Tereshkova. She had not been part of the original Russian cosmonaut training program, but had been recruited specially with this PR coup in mind. She had no previous piloting experience, though she was a keen free-fall parachutist. In fact, she was a textile worker, and had been one of the vast number of people who had written to apply to join the space program following Yuri Gagarin's first voyage into space.

Once again, the closeness of the orbits suggested an attempt at docking, though

OPPOSITE PAGE
Space flight piloted by the world's first woman cosmonaut Valentina Tereshkova on June 16, 1963.

THIS PAGE
The crew of *Voshkod 1*, October 12, 1964.

Tereshkova's lack of piloting expertise made this unlikely. Nevertheless, the two crafts were at one time only 3 miles (4.8 kilometers) apart, and there were occasions during the three days when both crafts were in orbit together, when an even closer rendezvous would have been possible. By this time, American plans for the Gemini two-man spacecraft were far advanced, although they had not followed the Russians in admitting women into their astronaut program, and they were confident they would soon take the lead in their orbital flights.

Unfortunately, again their hopes were to be ruined. Before the first Gemini flight, the Russians launched a large new spacecraft on October 12, 1964, carrying a crew of three. This was the *Voskhod 1*, an adapted Vostok weighing almost three-quarters of a ton more than its predecessor, and which was said to embody a number of improvements. It was the first spacecraft to use an ion engine, where a jet of charged particles (ions) and electrons is accelerated in an electric field and fired out into space, to produce a similar effect to a rocket engine, from a much lighter installation. It was also claimed that its reliability was good enough for the crew not to have to wear space suits aboard the craft, but the truth was that there was no room for these to be carried, and there was also no room for the parachutes needed for them to abandon the craft during the descent. Instead, by using special drogue parachutes and retro-rockets, the craft was brought down to a safe landing with the crew aboard.

The crew contained Konstantin Feoktistov, an engineer, Boris Yegorov who, as a physiologist, was able to address the concerns over space sickness shown on earlier missions by recording physical functions like blood pressure, muscle coordination, and samples of brain activity waveforms, and cosmonaut Vladimir Komarov, who was the commander of the mission. Because there was little room or spare payload weight for food, the flight had to be limited to just over a day in orbit.

The second Voskhod flight, launched on March 18, 1965, opted for greater endurance by only putting two men aboard, cosmonauts Alexei Leonov and Pavel Belyaev. In addition, some of the savings in weight and interior space were used to revert to carrying space suits, and also to install an air lock to allow the crew to move outside the craft while in orbit. So it was that on the day of the launch, Leonov climbed into his suit and inflated it to a low pressure of 6 pounds per square inch (0.42 kilograms per square centimeter), less than half the normal atmospheric pressure at sea level but which would allow him to maneuver inside the suit, in the vacuum of space.

Leonov went through the airlock and emerged for the first time on the outside of the spacecraft for the very first space walk. Although still tethered on a safety line, he was able to enjoy the sensations of floating free in weightless conditions, high above Earth, for minutes on end. He then tried to climb in through the hatch, but could only wriggle through the small opening by partially deflating his suit.

As if this wasn't enough to worry about, the crew then found the retro-rocket that was supposed to fire automatically to bring them out of orbit, failed to operate. The next opportunity for the crew to initiate the descent sequence themselves meant waiting for another orbit to be completed, but this would place the spacecraft off course because of the pattern traced by their flight over Earth's surface. When they eventually fired the rocket and the spacecraft came down to a successful landing, they were 2,000 miles (3,220 kilometers) away from the intended landing place, in the snow-covered Ural mountains where the rescue services took several hours to find them.

Problems like these made it clear that a new spacecraft was needed for more ambitious flights, and work began on the Soyuz spacecraft as a long-term objective. The Voskhod was retired after two launches, at the time when the Americans were perfecting their Gemini spacecraft. This had been tested by

GEMINI—TEST RUN FOR THE MOON

Unlike the Russians, who tended to see the best way of capitalizing on the prestige of their space program as producing a series of spectacular "firsts," the Americans soon switched to a longer-term view. Once President Kennedy had announced the target of a successful return trip to the Moon (see chap. 7), the American space program switched to a careful and painstaking process of developing and improving the techniques and technology needed to make the lunar expedition possible. This was the overriding aim of the Gemini program, and the frequency of their flights and the details of how they solved the problems they encountered on the way add up to one of the most awesome research projects ever attempted.

The third in the series of manned Gemini flights involved Pete Conrad and Gordon Cooper, launched on August 21, 1965 to practice docking maneuvers and test a new type of fuel cells. Unfortunately, the fuel cells malfunctioned, and by the time the problems had been solved, the crew encountered faults in the maneuvering rockets. Walter Schirra and Tom Stafford were due to carry out a planned rendezvous with an unmanned Agena spacecraft, launched by an Atlas rocket on August 25, 1965, but the launch failed, so the Gemini stayed on the ground.

By December 4, 1965, two Geminis were ready for launching. Frank Borman and James Lovell took the first one into space, with Schirra and Stafford following eleven days later. The two spacecraft actually maneuvered until only feet separated them, before Schirra and Stafford took their Gemini back to Earth after only a day in space. Borman and Lovell stayed in orbit for another two days to establish a new space endurance record of 330 hours.

Neil Armstrong and David Scott took another Gemini flight on March 16, 1966, when they were able at last to dock with a separately launched Agena spacecraft, for the first time ever. Unfortunately, one of the maneuvering rockets onboard the Gemini refused to shut down, causing the combination of the Gemini and the Agena to

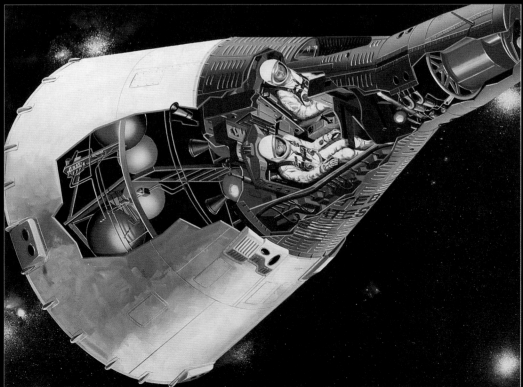

tumble out of control. The two astronauts had to disengage the two craft and then shut down the offending engine. By the time they had managed to do this, fuel was running low and the trip had to be cut short, after only eleven hours in space.

It was clear that the old days of one spectacular achievement after another were over. The Americans were painstakingly evolving an entirely new technology so that problems were solved one after the other, and new skills were learned that would one day make a moon flight possible. On June 3, 1966, Tom Stafford and Eugene Cernan took off to practice three rendezvous with another Agena. This time the Agena's docking mechanism jammed so that all they could do was practice the approaches to the target, and also undertake more ambitious space walks.

This time Cernan encountered the same problem as Leonov. After spending more than two hours in space, using a rocket pack on his back to control his movements, he found when he returned to the spacecraft that his exertions had tired him out.

During the next Gemini launch on July 18, 1966, eighth in the series of manned space flights, John Young and Michael Collins managed to dock successfully with two different Agena targets, and carry out a successful space walk, including a transfer between the Gemini and the Agena, and back. But when Richard Gordon tried a space walk from the ninth Gemini flight, he too suffered from complete exhaustion. The learning phase finally came to an end with the launch of *Gemini 12* on November 11, 1966. This was the tenth manned flight and involved James Lovell and Buzz Aldrin, and included another successful docking with an Agena, and the most successful space walk yet. Not only did Buzz Aldrin manage to use a set of tools to work on panels on the outside of the Gemini and on the inside of the docking adaptor, but by pacing his efforts, he avoided the fatigue and difficulty in climbing back aboard the spacecraft that his predecessors experienced.

OPPOSITE PAGE
Far left The *Gemini 4* launch in 1965.
Left An artist's concept of a two-man Gemini spacecraft in flight, showing a cutaway view.

THIS PAGE
Above Astronaut Edward H. White floats in zero gravity outside the *Gemini 4* spacecraft on June 3, 1965.
Below Gemini 6, taken from *Gemini 7* during rendezvous maneuvres.

two unmanned launches on April 8, 1964 and January 19, 1965, and the first manned launch took place just five days after Leonov and Belyaev's flight in *Voskhod 2*, on March 23, 1965.

The Gemini was a great improvement on its predecessor. Apart from being able to carry a two-man crew, it was a great deal more controllable, and the crew were able to practice the techniques and maneuvers needed to dock with other spacecraft. Virgil Grissom and John White stayed in orbit for almost five hours, making three circuits of Earth before descending to a splashdown in the ocean. They were followed on June 3, 1965, by James McDivitt and Ed White, who stayed in space for four days and sixty-four orbits. Not only did they try to rendezvous with the second stage of the *Titan II* rocket that launched them into orbit, but Ed White spent a total of twenty-one minutes in a space suit on the first American EVA (extra-vehicular activities, or

space walk) on orbit three, where he also tried out a handheld maneuvering gun. The Gemini program was now gathering pace.

By the time of its completion at the end of 1966, it would be time for both the Americans and the Russians to pause for breath before the next phase in manned space exploration. Both countries had new spacecraft under development. The Russian Soyuz spacecraft would be able to take more cosmonauts into space for longer and more ambitious orbital flights and to perform more varied and more complex experiments. But the Americans were also working on a new spacecraft that would carry three astronauts on a much more ambitious voyage altogether, and would end by putting their achievement on an even more spectacular plane than anything the Soviet Union had accomplished. The new spacecraft was the Apollo, and its destination was nothing less than the surface of the Moon.

THE FIRST CASUALTIES

Given the nature of the challenge, one of the most surprising factors in the early space flights was the excellent safety record. Yet at the time when both the Americans and Russians seemed to have put the early experimental phase behind them to enter on the well-understood practicalities of establishing space stations and journeying to and from the Moon, disaster struck. In the first case, involving three of the American pioneer astronauts, the spacecraft was not even in flight but down on the launching pad being checked in preparation for the initial launch.

This was the largest and most sophisticated spacecraft yet, the three-man Apollo that would eventually turn Moon trips into something of a routine. For the time being, though, it was essential to test every one of its systems, and on the late afternoon of January 27, 1967, Virgil Grissom, Ed White, and Roger Chaffee were aboard the capsule with the hatches closed and breathing pure oxygen, carrying out a series of checks.

The catastrophe struck with breathtaking speed. At 6:30 P.M. the instruments that

showed technicians outside the capsule the rate at which the oxygen was being used up showed a surge in the speed of consumption. At the same time, the monitor showing Ed White's heartbeat also showed a dramatic increase in speed, and within a minute the crew had reported a fire within the capsule and called to be let out.

With a bitter irony, it was the improvements to the design of the hatches following Virgil Grissom's splashdown in the ocean at the end of his Mercury flight that made this next to impossible. Instead of the original release handles, they now had to unfasten a set of bolts that could only be done from inside the capsule and that took more than a minute and a half. Before the crew could do this, the interior of the capsule was ablaze. The exterior skin became so hot that the emergency services took six minutes to force the hatch open, and by then all three occupants had burned to death.

Investigations showed that the interior of the capsule that had been supposed to take three men safely across a quarter of a million miles of space to the Moon and back, was a potential, and now an actual, death trap. There were three fatal flaws in its design and construction. First of all, the miles of electrical wiring had been badly fitted, with harnesses twisted round corners or left across surfaces where it was prone to damage. Second, the interior of the capsule had plastic materials that were not fire resistant, including netting and straps to hold objects under weightless conditions. Third, the pure oxygen atmosphere would turn the slightest spark into a furious blaze.

Almost certainly a stray spark from a defective or damaged section of wiring somewhere under Grissom's seat triggered the blaze. The result was a huge increase in pressure which split open the capsule from inside within seconds, after which the oxygen was consumed and the fire died down. Clouds of choking and lethal gas were produced by the burning plastic materials, and the fate of

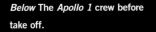

Below **The *Apollo 1* crew before take off.**

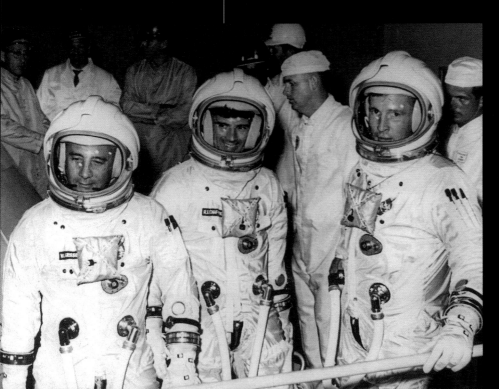

the astronauts was sealed. As a result, there was a radical redesign of the capsule, including thousands of modifications, a completely new hatch, revised wiring, and the use of fire-resistant plastics. This caused a delay of almost two years in the Apollo program, but resulted in a spacecraft that was a great deal safer for those who would travel in it. It was too late for poor Grissom, White, and Chaffee, and the tragedy took the lives of three men who had played a pioneering role in the whole space program, but at least the tragedy prevented a potentially more frightful disaster in the depths of space, where the causes might never have been revealed.

The final irony was that the Russians also suffered a fatal accident within three months of the Apollo fire, which killed one of their space pioneers. Vladimir Komarov was aboard *Soyuz 1*, the prototype of the Soviet Union's next-generation spacecraft, when it was launched on April 23, 1967, on a mission to dock with another spacecraft. He was the first Russian to make a second flight, but something had clearly gone badly wrong with the planned linkup, and on his eighteenth orbit he initiated the descent procedure for a return to Earth. The details were never revealed, but it was believed that the lines of

the parachute deployed to slow down his space capsule became entangled, and he was killed in the resulting crash. For both contenders in the space race, it was now clear that space itself was a very dangerous place.

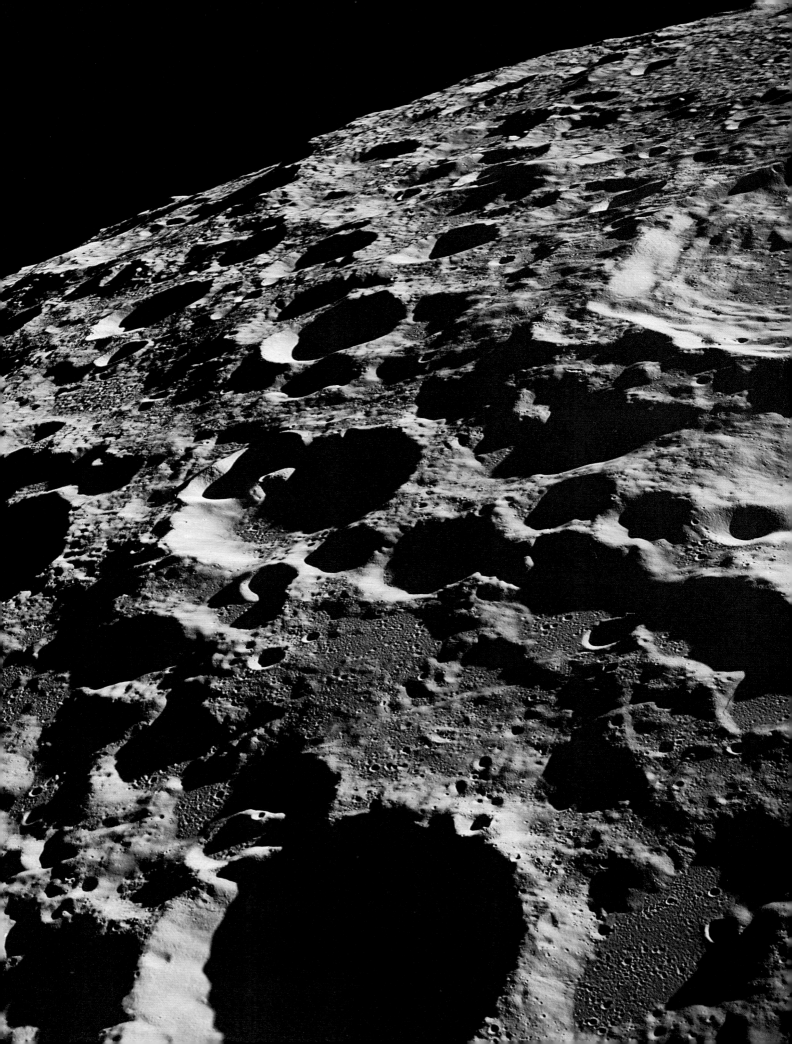

DESTINATION MOON

The story of the Apollo missions; the
technological advances made in the race to reach
the moon, the heroes, the disappointments, and
those first steps on the Lunar surface.

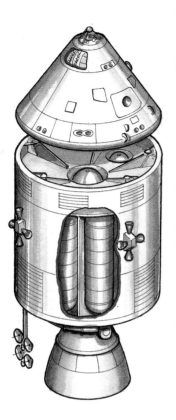

President John F Kennedy's target, announced on May 24, 1961, of putting a man on the Moon and bringing him back to Earth by the end of the decade, was a colossal gamble. At the time the pledge was made soon after his inauguration in a speech made to Congress, very little of the necessary technology even existed. There was no rocket powerful enough to lift the different parts of the spacecraft into Earth orbit, as the initial jumping-off point for the trajectory to the Moon. In addition there was no way of achieving a controlled landing on the lunar surface, let alone of taking off and returning to Earth.

To begin with, a much more powerful multistage rocket was needed, about ten times as powerful as its predecessors, to lift a minimum of 50 tons onto a trajectory for the Moon. This was to be the supreme achievement of von Braun's team. Their original *Saturn 1* was a powerful two stage liquid-fueled rocket, originally developed for military purposes, but which was still not powerful enough for the full moon-landing

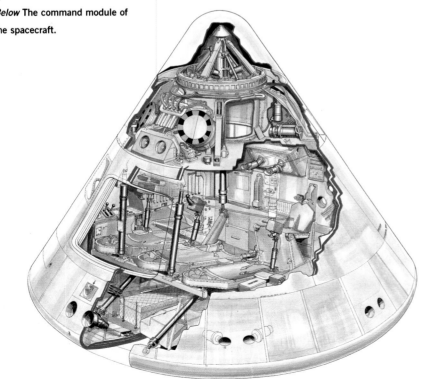

program. Nevertheless, it was capable of test-launching the Apollo spacecraft into Earth orbit flights. But for the complete journey, von Braun and his men would have to boost its power and endurance quite dramatically.

Their ultimate rocket was the *Saturn 5*, which stood a full 363 feet (110 meters) high, compared with the 224 feet (68 meters) of its predecessor. Its total thrust was no less than 744 tons. The first stage contained five rocket engines, burning kerosene and liquid oxygen, and strapped together inside a cylinder 33 feet (10 meters) in diameter and 138 feet (42 meters) in height. This would be sufficient to lift the payload needed to reach the Moon and return safely to a modest height of 37 miles (60 kilometers) above Earth's surface. Then the first stage would drop away, and the second stage would ignite. This was 81 feet (25 meters) high, and 33 feet (10 meters) across, containing five more rocket engines, this time burning liquid oxygen and liquid hydrogen. This would boost the spacecraft to a height of 100 miles (161 kilometers) above Earth before it too would be exhausted, and would drop away to save weight.

The third stage was slightly smaller but had a considerably more complex part to play in the whole project. It was 22 feet (6.7 meters) in diameter and 58 feet (18 meters) in height and it contained a single rocket, burning liquid hydrogen and liquid oxygen. Unlike the first and second stages, this had two different roles. Once the second stage had separated away, this third stage would boost the spacecraft into Earth orbit, and then be shut down. Though this sounds simple enough, it was the first time a liquid-fueled rocket would be shut down before burning all its fuel. Second, at the right moment in orbit to accelerate the spacecraft onto its precise trajectory for the Moon, it would need to be relit and deliver exactly the right amount of thrust for the right time to achieve that trajectory, within very fine limits.

However, when the spacecraft was in orbit it was weightless. Liquid fuel in partly filled tanks would not exert any pressure against the pumps, which normally forced them into the combustion chamber. To create this pressure, the designers fitted four reliable solid-fuel boosters that when fired would force the liquid fuels into the pumps and cause the main engine to take over. This would then boost the spacecraft to the speed needed to escape Earth orbit and head out across space to arrive in orbit around the Moon for the next stage of the journey.

The spacecraft itself consisted of several different sections, all linked together and weighing a total of 45 tons. The only part that would make the full round trip was the command module, effectively the conical nose of the rocket, measuring 12 feet (3.7 meters) in height and 13 feet (4 meters) in diameter and weighing four tons. Behind this was the

cylindrical service module, measuring 12 feet 9 inches (39 meters) in diameter and 22 feet (6.7 meters) long. This contained the propulsion system that allowed the astronauts to make any necessary corrections to their course when they were halfway to the Moon, retro-rocket power to slow down the craft into lunar orbit, and a rocket motor to leave lunar orbit and begin the journey back to Earth.

Behind this again was the lunar module, which would actually make the journey down to the Moon's surface. This was some 20 feet (6 meters) in height and 11 feet (3.3 meters) in diameter and weighed around 13 tons. It had two rocket engines, a descent engine with controllable thrust to allow a soft landing on the lunar surface, and a fixed-thrust ascent engine to power the module back into lunar orbit on the return trip. This was partly enclosed by the third stage of the Saturn rocket, but before it could be used to descend to the lunar surface it would need to be redeployed.

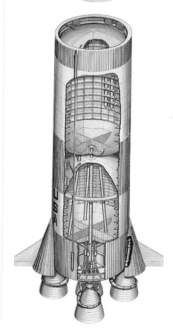

Left The lunar module with the lunar rover being deployed.
Right The enormous three-stage Saturn rocket

When the third stage of the *Saturn 5* had done its work and had been dropped, the lunar module would have to be detached from its position at the tail of the spacecraft. The astronauts would then have to turn around their command module and service module and then redock with the lunar module, with this now fixed to the nose of the conical command module instead of the tail end of the cylindrical service module.

Once they arrived safely in lunar orbit, the two astronauts who would descend to the surface, would scramble through the hatches into the lunar module, the hatches would be closed, and the connection severed. With the third astronaut remaining in orbit around the Moon aboard the command module, the lunar module would start its descent to the surface, using its own rocket engine to slow down to a smooth landing. When the exploration was complete, they would then climb back aboard the lunar module and fire its separate ascent engine, leaving behind the module's lower descent engine stage on the surface. The upper stage of the lunar module would climb back into lunar orbit, and then redock with the command module so that the astronauts could rejoin their colleague.

Once safely aboard the command module, the upper section of the lunar module would then be jettisoned in turn. At exactly the right moment, the rocket engine on the service module would be fired to accelerate the craft out of lunar orbit, on a trajectory for Earth. Once it arrived safely in Earth orbit the service module would be jettisoned, and the three astronauts would end their journey by splashing down in the ocean in the conical command module.

To do this they would have to turn the module around so that the heat shield on the base of the cone could absorb the huge temperature rise caused by friction with Earth's atmosphere during reentry. They also had to strike the atmosphere at the right angle for a successful reentry. Too steep a trajectory and the speed would rise too high. Too shallow a trajectory and the module would bounce off the upper layers of the atmosphere and ricochet back into space.

This was the theoretical program. However, in technological terms, much of this was unknown territory, and NASA knew very well that every part of the whole complex

Below The *J2* rocket motor, on exhibition in the United States.

routine would have to work perfectly if the project was not to end in tragedy and disappointment. The only sensible precaution was to test every part of the system and prove it would work perfectly when the occasion demanded, and the whole program was an object lesson in leaving as little as possible to chance.

Ironically, this careful test program was the reason why astronauts Gus Grissom, Ed White, and Roger Chaffee were on board the first Apollo capsule on January 27, 1967 when it caught fire (see chap. 6). The deaths of the three men exposed the need for a radical redesign of the capsule and undoubtedly improved the safety of the whole exercise, though it was a terrible reminder of the price to be paid for making mistakes.

The first systems to be tested were the different stages of the *Saturn 5* rocket itself. The *Saturn 1B* had been used to launch the unmanned *Apollo 1* spacecraft into Earth orbit as early as February 26, 1966. The first flight of the huge *Saturn 5* rocket, with the spacecraft aboard, took place on November 9, 1967, less than ten months after the fire disaster, and was a spectacularly ambitious undertaking. The flight was numbered 4 in the Apollo sequence and, like its predecessors, was unmanned.

Apollo 4 blasted off at seven o'clock in the morning local time from Cape Canaveral in Florida. The first stage dropped away, its fuel exhausted, followed by the second stage as the rocket performed exactly as intended. Finally the third stage fired and put the spacecraft

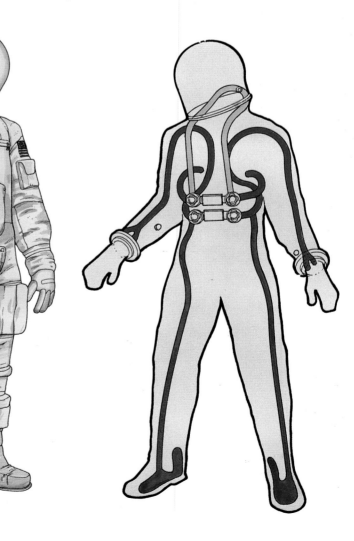

Below The "portable life-support system" for astronauts. Oxygen and power are supplied via the internal cords.

safely into Earth orbit, 115 miles (185 kilometers) up. So far, so good, but the critical phase was still to come. The new third stage engine would need to be restarted by ground signals since there was no one aboard to do the job. Would it work first time?

The signal was sent from Mission Control and the rocket motor ignited, exactly as planned. The third stage pushed the Apollo spacecraft into a much higher orbit, more than 10,000 miles (16,000 kilometers) from Earth. The next step was to test the spacecraft's own engines, so the third stage was jettisoned, and then the Apollo service module's engine was fired to boost the craft to a still higher orbit. Finally, the engine was used to put *Apollo 4* on trajectory for a return to Earth. The service module dropped away, and the unmanned command module made a perfect reentry and splashed down in the Pacific on schedule, just over eight and a half hours after launch.

It was a brilliant achievement, and showed that the objective of landing on the Moon was now a great deal more attainable than before. Unfortunately, the only part of the system that had not been tested on the *Apollo 4* flight was the lunar module itself. Even with the power of the *Saturn 5* to lift it onto a trajectory to the Moon, it was still necessary to save every pound of nonessential weight. The only way the lunar module could stay within weight limits was to design the landing legs to cope with the much weaker Moon gravity, but how could it be tested to show whether everything would work properly without actually taking it to the Moon?

Instead, *Apollo 5* was used to put the lunar module through its paces in orbit above Earth. The craft was launched on January 22, 1968, and once in orbit, its two engines were tested in turn. The descent engine was particularly important as this was the first time a rocket engine was built to be controllable within very fine limits. The astronauts would have to control the thrust of the descent engine from moment to moment, in a similar way to a

helicopter pilot using the upward thrust of the rotors, to effect a smooth and safe landing.

The descent engine worked exactly as intended. The ascent engine was simpler in its function but equally important, as this would be the astronauts only opportunity to leave the Moon and return to Earth. Unless the rocket delivered enough thrust to push their small and fragile craft back into lunar orbit at the same height as the command module, their chances of completing the mission would be almost zero. Happily for the Apollo project, this too worked perfectly.

The next step was to prove the whole launch system worked perfectly. *Apollo 6* was launched on a *Saturn 5* rocket on April 4, 1968, but hopes were blighted almost from the start. The first stage performed well and the second stage ignited as planned. Then the second stage died out prematurely and the third stage was forced to ignite earlier than intended. To the engineers' unbounded disappointment, this too failed to burn for the full time needed to place the spacecraft in Earth orbit. Worse again, it also failed to restart, to deliver the punch needed to put Apollo on course for the Moon.

The disappointment was intense, but the causes were clear. Instrument readings retrieved and analyzed at Mission Control showed a fuel leak had caused the first premature shutdown, and incorrect wiring was responsible for the subsequent faults. These could be corrected quickly, and the system should work as reliably as before.

For the moment, the question of the reliability of the *Saturn 5* had to be deferred, as the next step in the program was the manned test in Earth orbit of the command and service modules that would carry the astronauts to the Moon and back. Since this demanded less thrust than the full-scale Moon mission, the smaller *Saturn 1B* was used to launch the *Apollo 7* spacecraft on October 11, 1968, with Walter Schirra, Walter Cunningham, and Donn Eisels aboard. The smaller rocket performed faultlessly, and the module went

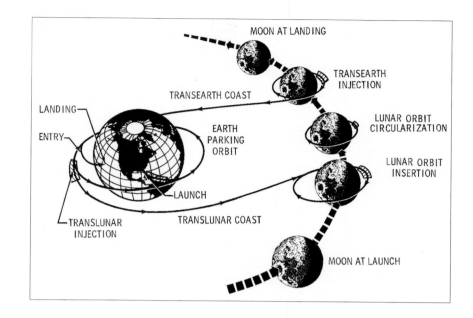

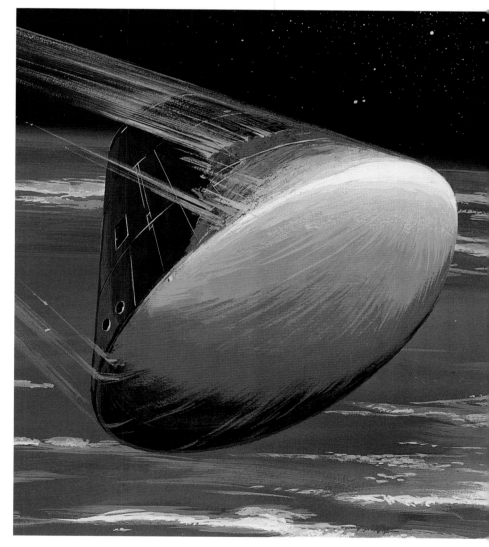

into Earth orbit for a total of 163 circuits. During this time, the astronauts were able to maneuver their craft to rendezvous with the rocket that had carried them, using the service module's own engine, and when they splashed down at the end of their mission, there only remained two links in the chain still yet to be proved: the *Saturn 5* after the rectification of the earlier faults and the lunar module with its crew on board.

At first, they intended to launch a new *Saturn 5* on December 1, 1968, to prove that all the different stages would fire properly, and then to launch a manned Apollo spacecraft with the lunar module aboard into Earth orbit on a *Saturn 1B*. By this time, the engineers were so confident that they decided to avoid some of the duplication, and to combine two

of the last steps in the program with a single stride. The launch of the *Saturn 5* was postponed for three weeks. When it did take off, it would be carrying *Apollo 8* and astronauts Jim Lovell, Frank Borman, and William Anders all the way to the Moon and back. For the first time, a manned space mission was leaving the confines of Earth behind.

Lovell, Borman, and Anders took off on their historic Moon flight just four days before Christmas 1968. The rocket worked perfectly, and after a single Earth orbit, they restarted the third stage engine for five minutes, to set a course for the Moon. For safety reasons, this initial course would allow them to simply curve around the Moon under the influence of lunar gravity for an automatic return to

OPPOSITE PAGE

Apollo 8 lift off.

THIS PAGE

The *Apollo 8* crew leaving
Kennedy Space Center before lift
off on December 21, 1968.

Earth if any major system failed. Only later, if all was well, would they fire the service module's engine to alter its course to pass within 70 miles (112 kilometers) of the Moon's surface.

Apollo 8 was captured by the Moon's gravitational pull, and settled into an elliptical orbit around it, by the astronauts turning the craft around and using its engine to slow them down. More engine corrections changed the orbit into a more circular path around the Moon, with an unparalleled view of its surface. After ten circuits, they fired the service module's engine again, to leave the Moon and head for Earth once more.

The rest of the flight, including the separation of the command module from the service module, and the reentry into the atmosphere at more than 6 miles (9.5 kilometers) per second, went equally smoothly, and *Apollo 8* splashed down into the ocean six days after launch. It was the best of omens for the future.

Only the manned lunar module test remained, and this was carried out in Earth orbit on a ten-day flight that began on March 3, 1969. At a height of almost 120 miles (193 kilometers), the astronauts separated the lunar module from the command module, then turned the command module around and linked it up to the lunar module. Astronauts James McDivitt and Russell Schweickart climbed into the lunar module and the two modules separated, leaving David Scott aboard the command module.

The lunar module was put through its paces, moving away to a distance of fifty miles (80 kilometers) and testing the engines and control systems before returning to the command module and linking up with it again. During the flight, they also tested new space suits, each carrying its own life-support system, that would be used on the lunar surface. Finally, with all three back on board the command module, the lunar module was jettisoned, and the command module with the three men aboard returned safely on March 13.

The nearest thing to a full dress rehearsal in the whole Apollo program was set for May 18, 1969. *Apollo 10,* with John Young, Tom Stafford, and Eugene Cernan on board, was launched on a flight that would approach closer to the Moon than even *Apollo 8* had done. They went through the same routine, but this time Stafford and Cernan climbed into the lunar module and using its descent engine for the first time over the Moon, sank slowly to a height of 8.9 miles (14,300 kilometers) over the planned landing site for *Apollo 11,* on the flat plain of the Sea of Tranquility. Then they climbed away to rejoin the command module and return to Earth. The next time men came to the Moon it would be to land on its surface.

One of the many anxieties facing the NASA planning teams was the nature of the Moon's surface. In particular, they needed to know what the lunar module would find as its supporting legs touched down. Would its feet land on solid rock, or would it be soft dust into which the feet might sink, allowing the module to tilt from the vertical and endanger its relaunch?

A whole series of Moon probes had been sent by both Russia and the United States (see chap. 9) but revealed little about the surface. Even *Ranger 9,* launched on February 17, 1965, which took thousands of pictures before it finally crashed into the Sea of Tranquility, failed to settle the question. Then the Russians launched *Luna 9* on January 31, 1966, which made the first soft landing in an area called the Ocean of Storms. The information it sent back showed the surface was stable, in that area at least.

The Americans achieved a similar feat when *Surveyor 1* made a soft landing on the lunar surface on June 2, 1966. This time the probe's landing feet were designed to place the same pressure on the surface as those of the lunar module, and a camera showed them in detailed close-up. The surface was hard enough to show only the faintest of marks, and later probes which dug into the surface to collect and analyze a sample of soil confirmed this good news.

THE EAGLE HAS LANDED

Apollo 11 extravehicular acitvity on the Moon.

THIS PAGE

Left A closeup view of an astronaut's foot and footprint in the lunar soil.

Right Astronaut Edwin E. Aldrin Jr., lunar module pilot, prepares to deploy the Early Apollo Scientific Experiments Package (EASEP) on the surface of the Moon.

The most vital Apollo mission of all, *Apollo 11*, was launched on July 16, 1969 with astronauts Neil Armstrong, Edwin "Buzz" Aldrin, and Michael Collins aboard. Once again, the launch, the flight into lunar orbit and the various maneuvers involved to reach that target went according to plan. Armstrong and Aldrin climbed into the lunar module Eagle, separated from the command module Columbia on the thirteenth lunar orbit, and started to descend to the lunar surface. This time they were going all the way.

Now the first warning signs appeared. Communications with Earth were patchy and messages had to be relayed through the command module. Huge amounts of information from the lunar module's instruments caused the Mission Control computer system to overload, and a warning light flashed. They decided this was an instrument failure rather than something more serious, and Eagle was told to make an automatically piloted landing.

Unfortunately, an otherwise trifling error in navigation had put the module four miles (6.5 kilometers) from the planned landing site, and it was approaching a field of large boulders which could cause damage. Neil Armstrong reported this to Mission Control and took over the landing manually. Slowly, softly and above all safely, Eagle landed on the lunar surface at 8:17 P.M. Greenwich Mean Time on July 20, 1969.

It took Armstrong and Aldrin more than six and a half hours to prepare the craft for the return journey, eat a meal, and climb into their space suits for their first walk on the lunar surface. After carefully walking down the ladder and taking his "small step for a man—one giant leap for mankind," Armstrong passed into the history books as the first human to reach the Moon. They spent two hours collecting 45 pounds (20.5 kilograms) of soil and rock samples, coming to terms with lunar gravity, and setting up a series of experiments, including a seismometer, equipment for measuring the solar wind, and a laser reflector to enable precise measurements of the distance between Earth and the Moon to be made.

After returning to the module, they then slept until it was time for the launch. At 6:03 A.M. Greenwich Mean Time on July 21, the ascent engine fired, and Eagle soared upward

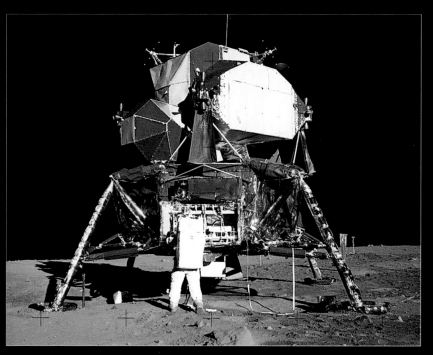

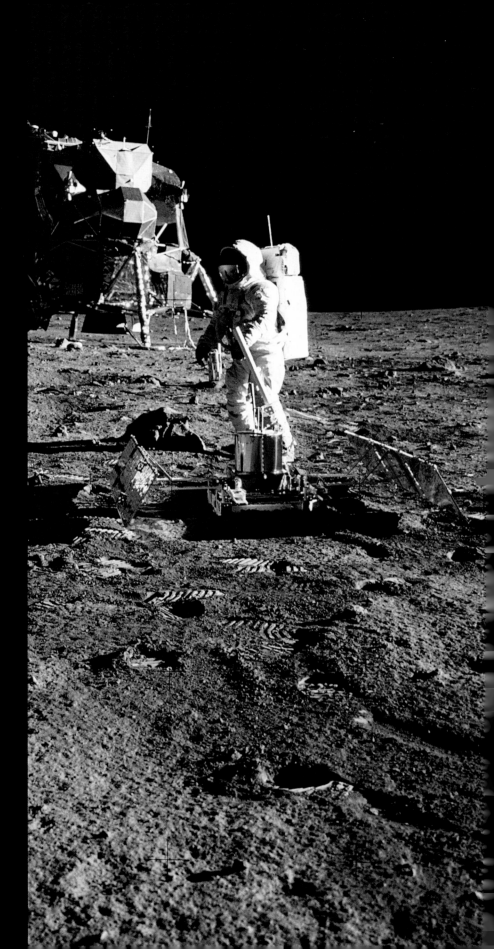

to rendezvous with Columbia after spending twenty-one hours and thirty-six minutes on the surface. In spite of difficulty during the final docking, the two craft linked up, the astronauts climbed back into the command module, and the lunar module was released. Ahead lay what was by now a perfectly routine flight back to Earth orbit, followed by reentry and splashdown in the Pacific Ocean on July 24, 1969. President Kennedy's promise had been kept.

Apollo 12 was launched on November 14, 1969. Richard Gordon remained in the command module, and Charles Conrad and Alan Bean landed in the Ocean of Storms on November 19, to make two Moon walks, set up a surface experiment, and collect 75 pounds (34 kilograms) of rock and soil samples.

Apart from *Apollo 13* the remarkable reliability and safety record of the Apollo flights was maintained to the end. After modifications were carried out, *Apollo 14* was launched on January 31, 1971. The lunar module landed in the Fra Mauro area of the Moon and once again the astronauts set up experiments, collected samples and returned to Earth on February 9, 1971.

Later that same year on July 26, *Apollo 15* went to the Hadley Rille area, near the lunar Apennine Mountains, where astronauts David Scott and James Irwin landed in the lunar module and Alfred Worden stayed in the command module. This was the first outing for the four-wheeled battery-powered lunar roving vehicle, which greatly increased their range.

Apollo 16 was launched on April 16, 1972, taking astronauts John Young and Charles Duke to the Moon's Descartes Highlands. Finally, on December 7, 1972, *Apollo 17* left on the last flight of this amazing series, heading for the edge of the Sea of Serenity, near the crater Littrow. The flight broke all the previous records for the time spent on the Moon, the distance traveled by lunar rover, and the bringing back of more than 250 pounds (113 kilograms) of samples.

Far left and above left
Aldrin preparing to deploy the
Early Apollo Experiments Package.
Bottom left The three *Apollo 11*
crew members await pickup by a
helicopter from the USS *Hornet*.
Above The moon.

With the careful premission test program successfully completed, and the outstanding success of *Apollo 11* and *Apollo 12* to point the way, there seemed nothing particularly unusual about the launch of *Apollo 13*. Astronauts Jim Lovell, John Swigert, and Fred Haise were heading for the Fra Mauro region (later to be explored by *Apollo 14*). All went well past their ejection from Earth orbit onto their trajectory for the Moon.

Just past the midcourse correction point, disaster struck. One of the liquid-oxygen tanks in the service module exploded, and it was quickly clear that both of the spacecraft's power supplies were in trouble. One had failed and the other was showing signs of following suit. The only other power source was the batteries aboard the command module to be used during reentry.

The implications were terrifying. Power was needed for heating, light, life support, instruments, and all the other vital functions to keep the astronauts and the spacecraft alive. The immediate priority was to get the spacecraft back to Earth as quickly as possible. Short of turning it around and reversing its course, which would have demanded large amounts of energy, the most practical

Above and right **Different views of the severely damaged *Apollo 13* service module taken by a Maurer motion picture camera from the lunar module.**

alternative seemed to be to correct its course so that it could swing around the Moon before heading home. Unfortunately, there was no way that the power and life-support systems in the service module could last that long.

The solution to the problem was to use the lunar module as a space lifeboat. Since this had its own independent power and life-support systems for the lunar landing, they could endure for a much longer time. The astronauts had to augment the water supplies by bailing water from the command module tank using plastic bottles, and they rerigged air supply connections using adhesive tape and plastic sheet. Meanwhile, the command module's battery power was saved by using the lunar module engines to carry out the maneuvering to correct their course on the way back to Earth.

By the time they approached reentry, the crew were suffering from cold, fatigue, and dehydration. In this state it was all too easy to make mistakes. When they dropped the service module, they were appalled to see the size of the hole blown in the side by the exploding tank, and when they powered up the command module batteries, they were shocked to see that the current was draining out far too quickly.

Only when communications were reestablished and the circuits turned on did they find that a switch had been left on. The crew transferred to the command module, set up the computer for reentry, and the lunar module that had saved their lives was finally jettisoned, to drop away into the ocean. Their final worry was the trajectory taken up by the spacecraft, which was perilously close to bouncing away into space. When Mission Control checked, they found the error had been caused by water boiling off the cooling system on the lunar module. Once that was dropped, the service module remained only just within the limits for a successful reentry and splashdown. The Apollo safety record had held, but only barely.

Left Recovery of the *Apollo 13* astronauts, aided by underwater demolition team swimmers. *Below* Commander R. E. Jerauld offers a prayer of thanks for the safe return of the *Apollo 13* crew members.

REUSABLE ROCKET: THE SPACE SHUTTLE

A new era in space travel was boosted into the heavens with the launch of the space shuttle, laying the foundations for long-term space exploration.

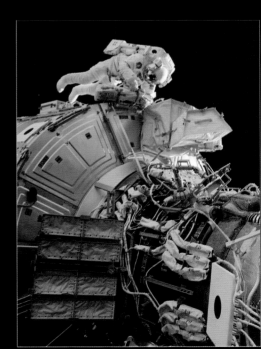

For the Americans, and for NASA in particular, the main problem of the Moon landings had been their success. Having invested enormous efforts and resources to put the astronauts on the surface of Earth's only satellite, and to bring them back safely, there was a real danger that the space program had nowhere else to go. Extending the reach of the manned-landing program to the next logical planetary objective of Mars was out of the question, on the grounds of cost and the timescale involved. Maintaining a program of unmanned probes would be infinitely cheaper and easier to carry out, and would undoubtedly result in an increase in our knowledge of the solar system, and the wider universe, but it lacked the vital human-interest quality to attract the budgetary backing that NASA needed.

The solution to the problem proved to be a return to the home pastures of Earth orbit, where a whole series of new challenges awaited. By using a succession of flights to construct a space station, it would be possible to carry out valuable long-term experiments in a weightless environment, and possibly lay the first foundations of future longer-distance space flights. But before any of this could take place, another technological obstacle barred the way.

The Saturn rocket had made the Moon landings possible, but it was a horrifically expensive way to launch men and materials into space, since most of each rocket, costing U.S.$120 million each at the time, was effectively thrown away after one use. What they now needed was a reusable space launch vehicle that could be brought back to Earth at the end of each mission to be refueled and serviced, and then used again, as often as was necessary. This would cut the cost of space travel by a whole order of magnitude, and essential for NASA's future prospects.

Before the technology questions could be solved, NASA faced new problems. The space station project was rejected by the U.S. Senate, and on the face of it, there was now no need for a reusable manned launch vehicle, since

only unmanned satellites and space probes would represent the future of space research. Yet the very importance of satellites was finally to guarantee the viability and usefulness of the development that would eventually produce the space shuttle. Since it would reduce the cost of launching human astronauts into orbit, it would also make satellite launches cheaper and more reliable. Indeed, it would even make it possible to service and repair existing satellites, and to extend their operational life many times over.

In some respects, the task of developing a shuttle vehicle was more difficult and less straightforward than producing a powerful and reliable rocket. By the late 1960s, rocket technology was well understood, and the problems of providing accurate control systems which would work within the atmosphere and in the depths of space had been solved. However, the only way of making a vehicle which could return to Earth at the end of its trip meant producing what was, in effect, a space-going aircraft that could fly in the ordinary way once it reentered the atmosphere.

Just as with the moon-landing project, a series of logical decisions shaped the basic design of the space shuttle. In this case, though, some time was wasted in following

what turned out to be a blind alley. The Americans had a great deal of useful experience in operating rocket-propelled aircraft in the upper layers of the atmosphere, from the development of experimental research planes in the X-series. These were slung below a conventional bomber, which flew to its highest operating altitude before launching the rocket-propelled craft.

In the thin layers of the upper atmosphere, these planes could reach prodigious speeds. The *X-1*, launched in 1947, was the first aircraft to break through the so-called sound barrier into supersonic flight, and the *X-15* was capable of a maximum speed of 4,000 miles per hour (6,430 kilometers per hour). Later, the Americans experimented with aircraft that

By January 1986, twenty-three more Shuttle flights had succeeded the successful first launch, and the program was becoming almost routine. There were now four shuttles, *Atlantis, Columbia, Discovery,* and *Challenger,* and during the year it was planned to use the craft on no less than thirteen missions, ranging from the launch of communications and secret military satellites to experiments for materials scientists and drug manufacturers. The first of these missions involved *Challenger,* which was standing on the launching pad ready for liftoff on January 28, carrying a full complement of five men and two women, one of them a thirty-seven-year-old teacher named Christa McAuliffe, who was to be the first private citizen to be carried into space as a public relations gesture from NASA to help popularize missions, which were generating less interest than the moon flights.

The launch appeared to go according to plan, and the main engines fired on schedule, closely followed by the solid fuel boosters. *Challenger* rose off the launch pad on the usual awesome pillar of fire from the battery of rocket motors. Five seconds after lifting off, *Challenger* rolled into the climb attitude and the ascent continued. Within just over a minute the craft had reached an altitude of 50,000 feet (15,240 meters). Another minute would see the exhausted booster rockets drop away, their duty done. But something was going terribly, fatally wrong.

Just seventy-four seconds into the flight, the huge external tank strapped to the underside of the *Challenger* orbiter suddenly exploded with terrifying force, blowing the craft to pieces. The two boosters, still firing normally, continued upward, corkscrewing into the sky from a total lack of any control. The mission was over before it had begun, and the seven people aboard could never have known what was happening.

NASA mounted an exhaustive inquiry to determine what had caused the disaster, and in the meantime the remaining shuttle flights were canceled. The fault was eventually traced to flawed seams in the booster rocket casings that had allowed jets of burning fuel to play on the tail end of the fuel tank, finally raising its temperature to explosion point. Eventually, the shuttle flights were resumed after a two year delay in 1988, and a new shuttle, the *Endeavor,* was completed in 1991.

Below Different stages of the *Challenger* disaster, starting with the first indication of smoke, up to the actual explosion, seconds after launch.

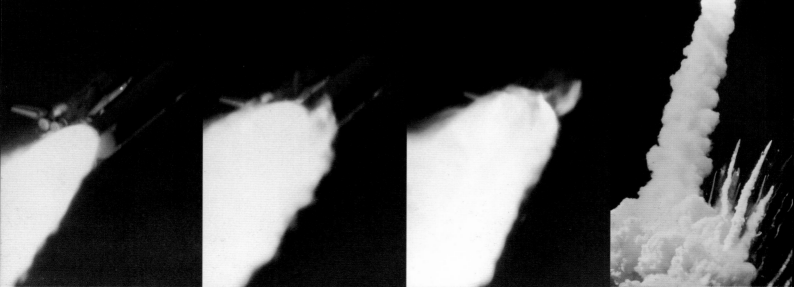

Right The *Challenger* crew members who lost their lives on January 28, 1986. From left to right, front row Michael J. Smith, Francis R. Scobee, Ronald E. McNair and behind Ellison S. Onizuka, Sharon Christa McAuliffe, Gregory Jarvis, and Judith A. Resnik.
Right An expanding ball of gas from the external tank creates a plume of white cloud in the sky.

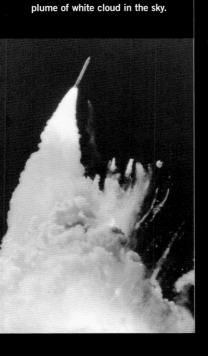

could reach even higher speeds, but these had to be launched to their operating altitude by a booster rocket like the Atlas. In the circumstances, it was perhaps hardly surprising that NASA should have considered that the way forward was to use a rocket to provide the sheer power to launch the shuttle into orbit, but to have a pilot on board so that it too could return to Earth for a safe landing before it was refueled and launched again.

This idea was ditched fairly early in the program. By 1971, it had been decided that the only piloted part of the shuttle vehicle would be the orbiter. To launch this into orbit around Earth would call for a pair of solid-fuel rocket boosters that would drop off when their fuel was exhausted, in the same way as the first stage of a rocket. However, these boosters would carry parachutes that would allow them to drop back to the surface slowly enough for them to be retrieved, refilled, and reused for a whole series of launches. The orbiting shuttle itself would continue to ascend on its three main engines, supplied with their fuel of liquid oxygen and liquid hydrogen from a huge fuel tank strapped below the orbiter.

Once the shuttle approached its orbiting height, the main tank would be jettisoned and would fall back through the atmosphere, breaking up as it did so, ultimately falling into the ocean, the only major part of the shuttle design which would not be reusable. For the rest of its flight, the shuttle would rely on its own internal maneuvering engines. These would also be used to slow down the craft when it was time to return to Earth.

In many ways, the most difficult design objective was making sure the shuttle could survive reentry into the atmosphere and remain controllable right down to a normal aircraft-type approach and landing. The huge heat buildup during reentry called for very effective protection, especially around key areas, like the leading edges of the stub wings and the nosecap of the orbiter.

The wings themselves were another area of possible weakness. The United States had

experimented with high-altitude research aircraft that had no wings at all, where the body itself was shaped to operate like an aerofoil and generate its own lift, but this type of aircraft could not be controlled at reasonable speeds in the lower, denser layers of the atmosphere. Wings would be needed, and these had to be made as large as possible to allow sufficient control for a safe landing at a speed that would be low enough to allow the shuttle to be brought to rest within the confines of a specially lengthened runway. On the other hand, over-large wings would be vulnerable at reentry, and might even be torn away when they encountered the atmosphere on the return journey from space.

In the end, the small delta wings and tailfin fitted at the rear end of the shuttle

OPPOSITE PAGE
Astronaut Bruce McCandless II, conducts a simulation of a chore scheduled on a later mission to aid the damaged Solar Maximum satellite.

THIS PAGE
The successful capture of the *Intelsat VI* satellite is recorded over Mexico from the shuttle's *Endeavor* cabin.

THE SHUTTLE AT WORK

In order to enable the Shuttle to launch satellites into higher, geostationary orbits, engines were developed to be attached to the satellites, to propel them from the cargo bay to the correct height. The first of these was the 20 ton Interim Upper Stage engine (IUS) which could lift a 2.5 ton satellite into geostationary orbit. For satellites of smaller sizes and weights, different Payload Assist Modules were developed to do the job instead.

Because there was a definite limit on the size of experiments that could be carried out within the restricted space of the two-deck pressurized cabin of the orbiter, the European Space Agency developed the Spacelab project, a form of semi-space station built up of different modules. These modules were designed to fit within the Shuttle's cargo bay, and could be used for a wide variety of different experiments.

By the time of the fifth shuttle launch in November 1982, the craft was ready to embark on a commercial project. Once established in orbit, it boosted two communications satellites into higher orbits, according to plan. Unfortunately, events did not always run so smoothly. On a mission in April 1983, the IUS launching NASA's own Tracking and Data Relay Satellite (TDRS) space communications failed to function properly, leaving the satellite at too low an altitude, and only the careful work of ground controllers, issuing commands to the satellite's own stabilization thrusters, succeeded in being pushed to the required height.

A more successful mission was mounted in April 1984, the eleventh in the series, to repair the Solar Maximum Mission satellite, an Earth-orbiting space observatory launched in 1980. In this case, the crew were able to extend the controllable robot arm of the orbiter, to capture the satellite and transfer it into the cargo bay, where repairs were made before it was relaunched into orbit. Later that year, the astronauts were able to use a jet-powered backpack called the Mobile

Maneuvering Unit (MMU) that allowed them to move away from the orbiter, under their own power, to a maximum range of some 300 feet (91 meters), without any line to tether them to the craft.

In more recent years, the shuttle has been used to repair the Hubble space telescope, that was originally suffering from blurred images, caused by faults in the computer-controlled grinding of the telescope's primary mirror. Launched on December 2, 1993, the shuttle *Endeavor* made a successful rendezvous with the telescope, and the team of four astronauts was able to install an ingenious ten mirror array to correct the vision of the main mirror, together with a new wide-field planetary camera. They also replaced the telescope's faulty gyroscopes and worn solar panels, and their efforts enabled the Hubble telescope to produce some truly stupendous images of the previously unseen older and more distant parts of the universe.

Although criticisms have been made that the cost of launching satellites with the shuttle is actually higher than using once-only rockets, once the enormous costs of its development are included, the project made possible a wide variety of experiments and missions that would not have been possible in any other way. Significantly, a number of projects are underway for new low-cost launch systems, like the reusable launch vehicle (RLV) which would take off vertically and land horizontally like the shuttle, but would be different in three important ways. It would be unmanned, it would use metallic heat shields instead of the silica tiles of the shuttle, and it would carry its boosters and fuel tanks with it instead of dropping them during the climb into orbit.

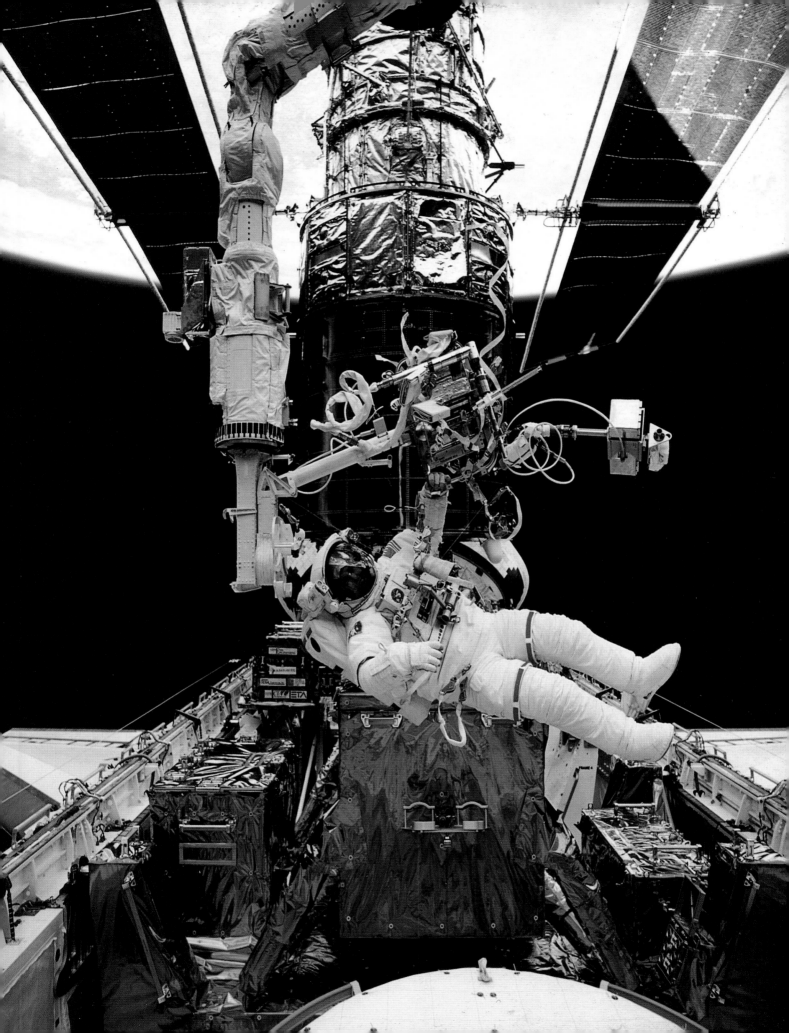

would prove to be strong enough to cope with reentry, and to allow the pilot to bring down the craft in an accurate approach to allow a touch-down at a blistering 200 miles per hour (322 kilometers per hour), on a special runway at Edwards Air Force Base in California's Mojave Desert. However, the protection against the soaring temperatures of reentry proved much more of a problem.

The cause was the difficulty of persuading a layer of specially developed thermal insulating tiles to stick to the underside of the craft. These black tiles were capable of standing up to temperatures in the region of 2,172 degrees Fahrenheit, which would be experienced on reentering the atmosphere, and the material itself was reliable enough. Similar white tiles were fixed to the shuttle's upper surfaces for lower temperature insulation, while reinforced carbon composite tiles were fixed to the high-stress areas of the leading edges of the wings.

Unfortunately, the curves and edges of the craft's surface caused a problem for the adhesive used to fix the tiles. Tiles dropped off with depressing frequency, and the problem was not entirely solved by the time the rest of the design and development program had been completed, and the first space shuttle *Columbia* was ready to fly on April 10, 1981.

By the time the first shuttle had actually been built, it was clearly a promising and versatile craft, a curious combination of space vehicle and conventional aircraft. The flight-deck, situated in the upper section of the nose, has two seats set side-by-side, for the mission commander and the pilot who controls the craft. Behind them are two more seats for a mission specialist and the astronaut in charge of the payload carried on each particular flight. Below the flight deck is a mid-deck with seats for up to three more passengers, crew bunks, a galley, and a central air lock to allow the crew access to the unpressurized central cargo bay which carries the main mission payload. Below the mid-deck is a lower deck that is used as an equipment bay, with room for lockers, space suits and life support systems for the crew.

The most important part of the whole shuttle craft is the cargo bay, since this is the real reason for the entire project. It measures 60 feet (18 meters) long by 15 feet (4.5 meters) wide and is closed off by two large doors that can be opened and closed in orbit. The mathematics of the launch system make it possible to carry objects weighing up to almost thirty tons into low Earth orbit, and correspondingly lighter loads into higher trajectories. This allows up to four communications satellites to be carried in the

OPPOSITE PAGE

Top Discovery's cargo bay with the air lock clearly open nearby.
Bottom Challenger's extensive cargo bay.

THIS PAGE

Below Astronaut Claude Nicollier prepares a meal for himself at the galley on *Columbia's* mid-deck.
Below right The special tiles used in the construction of the shuttle.

bay at one time, each one with its own booster to fire it even higher, to the altitude needed for a geosynchronous orbit. It is also fitted with a controllable arm which can be used to retrieve existing satellites from orbit and place them into the cargo bay for repair and maintenance to be carried out.

The shuttle's enticing future prospects still remained unrealized when the countdown for the first launch was interrupted, after two days of delays, while various malfunctions were identified and cured with just nine minutes to go, due to an apparent computer problem. Four of the five computers controlling the launch were working normally, but the fifth was failing to exchange data with the others. The problem

was finally traced to a lack of synchronization between the internal clocks controlling the different computers, and the launch was rescheduled for April 14, 1981.

Finally, at seven in the morning of a spring Sunday, the countdown was complete. With exactly 3.8 seconds to go, the onboard computers triggered the ignition of the first main engine, followed at intervals of approximately one-eighth of a second each, the lighting of main engines two and three. As the thrust delivered by these three engines increased to the point where they were lifting the two thousand tons of *Columbia* off the launchpad, the launch control system fired the two solid-fuel boosters, and the bolts holding

the whole assembly to the pad were detonated. The huge shuttle assembly blasted off into the heavens, driven upward by the enormous thrust of five rocket engines.

Then followed a complex series of maneuvers. Just five seconds after liftoff, *Columbia* rolled through 120 degrees to place the huge fuel tank uppermost. After two minutes and twelve seconds the two boosters detached and fell away, their fuel exhausted. Six minutes later and *Columbia* reached the peak of its first climb, at an altitude of 81 miles (130 kilometers), before descending to a height of 72 miles (116 kilometers), where the main fuel tank was dropped. With that falling away safely, *Columbia's* maneuvering engines were restarted to boost the craft into an operating orbit. On this first flight it was approximately 170 miles (273 kilometers) above the surface of Earth, but future missions could reach altitudes of between 115 and 690 miles (185 and 1,110 kilometers), depending on the needs of the particular mission being flown.

In the case of the historic first flight of *Columbia*, the time in orbit was used to check the craft's operating systems, and particularly the tiles and the cargo bay doors. Finally, the crucial preentry maneuvers were carried out. First the shuttle had to be turned around so that the main maneuvering engine could be fired to slow it down and drop it out of orbit over the Pacific. Then *Columbia* had to be turned around again into the correct attitude for reentry, facing forward in the direction of flight, and the right way up.

For the approach to the landing field at Edwards Air Force Base the pilot, John Young, flew the Shuttle like a huge and complex glider, carrying out a series of S-turns to lose speed and height before making his final approach. The entire Shuttle craft was designed to be landed successfully first time, since the power and control systems would not allow the possibility of an overshoot followed by repositioning for a second landing. Fortunately for the crew and the future of the

shuttle project, everything went according to plan. Young had *Columbia* lined up on the glide path well in advance. All that remained was to fly the craft exactly on trajectory until it was almost touching the ground as it swept over the beginning of the runway. A slight back pressure on the control column lifted *Columbia's* nose in a perfect flare, and the craft settled back onto its main landing gear at 200 miles per hour (320 kilometers per hour). As the pilot braked it to a stop, it was clear that the future of manned space flight was shuttle shaped.

Below Almost routine—space shuttle launch, 1980s.

Left Astronaut Bruce McCandless II is pictured on the manned maneuvering unit above earth on February 7, 1984.
Below An artist's concept depicting the de-orbit burn before returning to make its runway landing like a conventional aircraft.
Bottom A front view showing *Columbia's* touchdown at Kennedy Space Center's landing facility.

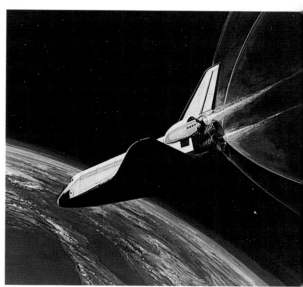

THE OTHER SPACE SHUTTLE

OPPOSITE PAGE
Buran being carried by *Energiya* in flight, May 19, 1989.

THIS PAGE
The *Energiya* booster rocket with *Buran* on the launch pad.

If imitation is the sincerest form of flattery, then the best evidence that the Americans had made the correct decision when they designed the space shuttle, and its supporting systems, was provided by its Soviet equivalent. In 1978, Russian scientists and engineers began working on a project coded VKK (the initials stood for the Russian equivalent of Air-Space Vehicle System), which was to consist of the huge Energiya rocket, and a reusable shuttle-type hybrid space vehicle/aircraft.

The whole setup looked like a clone of NASA's Shuttle and its main rocket, though there were detail differences. The Russian shuttlecraft, named *Buran*, had maneuvering engines but no main engine, since the power would be provided by the main *Energiya* booster, with its thrust of 3,500 tons, or approximately the same as the *Saturn 5* Apollo moon rocket. In addition, there was no need for separate twin boosters and a main tank, since the rocket combined both functions with four strap-on boosters and a second stage that were jettisoned during the ascent.

Because of the power of the rocket, the first test launch on May 15, 1987 resulted in damage from its own rocket blast as *Energiya* lifted off the pad. In order to prevent this happening again, a concrete flame pit five stories deep was dug in the center of the launchpad to absorb the fury of the rocket exhaust and channel it away through three separate vents. The crews of *Buran* boarded their craft through a tubular walkway from a specially protected bunker, and in an emergency would be able to slide back down an escape chute into the bunker in seconds.

The first flight of *Buran* took place on November 15, 1988, but was carried out without a crew, operating under automatic control. The *Energiya* rocket lifted the shuttle into initial Earth orbit at a height of 99 miles (160 kilometers). The shuttle's own maneuvering engines boosted the craft to a height of 155 miles (250 kilometers) for two complete orbits. *Buran* was then turned around and the maneuvering engine fired to slow down the craft and initiate its return to Earth's atmosphere.

At a height of 25 miles (40 kilometers), the spacecraft began its controlled glide toward a specially laid-out airstrip close to the Baikonur launch site, where it successfully touched down, still under automatic control, after a flight of three hours twenty-five minutes. The Soviet Union announced a program of four shuttle flights a year, but this seems to have been dropped in favor of continuing with conventional rocket launches, though it was intended that *Buran* and its successors would play a vital part in any planned mission to send cosmonauts to Mars.

SPACE STATIONS

From the unmanned Orbiting Solar Observatories to the multiple docking and extensively automated Mir station, the concept of exploring space from an outpost has been hugely significant in the development of our knowledge of outer space.

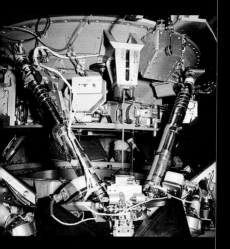

With improving relations between Russia and the United States, more information had been shared between the scientists working on space programs in both countries. One valuable area of cooperation included possible rescue of spacecraft in difficulties, which meant the development of a compatible docking system. This project began in 1970, and five years later resulted in an Apollo spacecraft docking in Earth orbit with a Soyuz, in July 1975, where the astronauts were able to move between two spacecraft and conduct joint scientific experiments.

This was a far more complex operation than it appeared, since it was not only the docking fittings and procedures that had to b modified, but the composition and pressure o the atmosphere within American and Russian spacecraft, to make them more compatible. Ir addition, the Soyuz had to be given a green and white color scheme to make it easier to see against the background of space, as painting it white all over, like the American spacecraft, would have a drastic effect on the internal temperature. This careful work helpec pave the way for the much more ambitious cooperative missions on the Mir space station, and made possible the development of the even more ambitious International Space Station (see chap. 12).

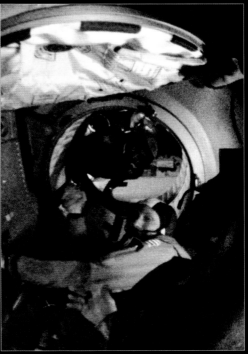

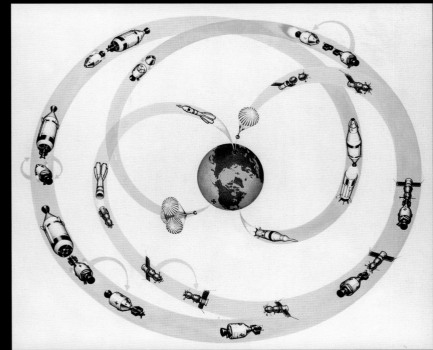

OPPOSITE PAGE

Far left top Junior researcher Y.G. Pobrov observes testing of the Apollo-Soyuz docking system at Rockwell International's plant in Downey, California.

Left Soviet Soyuz spacecraft photographed from a rendezvous window of the American Apollo in Earth orbit.

THIS PAGE

Top An illustration of a future concept for a space station.

Above An artist's concept of the mission profile of the Apollo-Soyuz Test Project, including launch, rendezvous, docking, separation, and splashdown.

Above left Astronaut Thomas P. Stafford (front) and cosmonaut Aleksei A. Leonov make their historic handshake in space on July 17, 1975.

Above The Apollo Telescope Mount (ATM) is featured in this artist's concept of the Skylab cluster.

Right An illustration showing a cutaway view of the *Skylab 1* Orbital Workshop (OWS), one of the five major components of the space station.

Even before *Apollo 11* landed in the Sea of Tranquility, many scientists argued that this was an impossibly complex and expensive way to explore space. Better by far, in their opinion, was the relatively simpler, and much less costly task of building and establishing space stations in Earth orbit, where astronauts could explore the conditions of living in space for long periods, and carry out a wide variety of experiments in a weightless environment.

In the longer term, space stations might even help make interplanetary travel possible. Building spacecraft capable of reaching the nearer planets like Mars and Venus would be a great deal easier if they could be assembled outside Earth's atmosphere. Without the stresses and strains of being launched from the surface, and without the need for the still more immense rockets that would be required to boost an interplanetary spacecraft free of Earth's gravity, the task of developing long-distance spacecraft would become more feasible in theory, if not more affordable in practice.

In reality, the space station concept began at an early stage in space exploration. On March 7, 1962, less than five years after *Sputnik 1*, the United States launched the first of a whole series of orbiting solar observatories, effectively unmanned space stations that monitored solar activity. By 1975, eight of these unmanned orbiting observatories kept a close watch on our nearest star. Together with a series of orbiting geophysical observatories, orbiting astronomical observatories, and the Soviet elektron, proton, and prognoz series of satellites, launched from 1964 into the late 1980s, these unmanned space stations produced a wealth of scientific information.

The first manned space stations appeared after the successful Apollo moon landings, though the Russians were first off the mark. Their first space station, *Salyut 1*, was launched on April 19, 1971, without a crew. Its maneuvering engine was mounted at the lower end, with a docking port at the upper end, and a pair of solar panels at either end, opening out to generate power once the craft was safely established in orbit.

Four days later *Soyuz 10* carried three cosmonauts into orbit. Their task was to test the new system to link the hydraulic and electrical circuits of both craft as part of the docking process. Once docking was completed, the two craft separated again after two days in space. The Soyuz returned to Earth, and the Salyut remained in orbit with no one on board, waiting for the next crew to arrive.

On June 6, 1971, another three astronauts, Georgi Dobrovolsky, Vladislav Volkov, and Viktor Patsayev approached the space station, under automatic control, aboard *Soyuz 11*. When these were within 330 feet (100 meters) of Salyut, they continued under manual control until the two craft made contact and the docking was completed. They then wriggled through the connecting tunnel at the top of their spacecraft to board the space station for the first time. There they carried out a wide range of experiments, including a series of plant-growth trials to develop food for long-term space flights. Once their program was complete, they returned to their Soyuz capsule for their journey back to Earth.

It was on this most routine part of the mission that disaster struck. Because of limited space, the crew were not able to wear space suits aboard Soyuz. Unfortunately, during the reentry into Earth's atmosphere, the pressure equalizing valve in the docking system malfunctioned, allowing the cabin air to escape into space. The craft's parachutes deployed automatically, and the capsule came down to a perfect landing, but when the ground recovery crews opened the hatches, they found the entire crew was dead.

Apart from the individual tragedy, there was a danger the problem might recur on future flights to the station. On October 11, 1971, after 175 days in orbit, Soviet Mission Control turned *Salyut 1* around and fired its maneuvering engine to slow it down. This caused it to lose altitude and finally break up on reentry over the vast spaces of the Pacific. The first manned space station had been both promising and disappointing, in equal measure.

Salyut 2, was launched almost eighteen months later, on April 3, 1973. Within

Below This artist's concept shows the Skylab space station cluster in Earth orbit. The cluster is composed of the Apollo Command/Service Module, Orbital Workshop, Apollo Telescope Mount, Multiple Docking Adapter, and Air Lock Module.

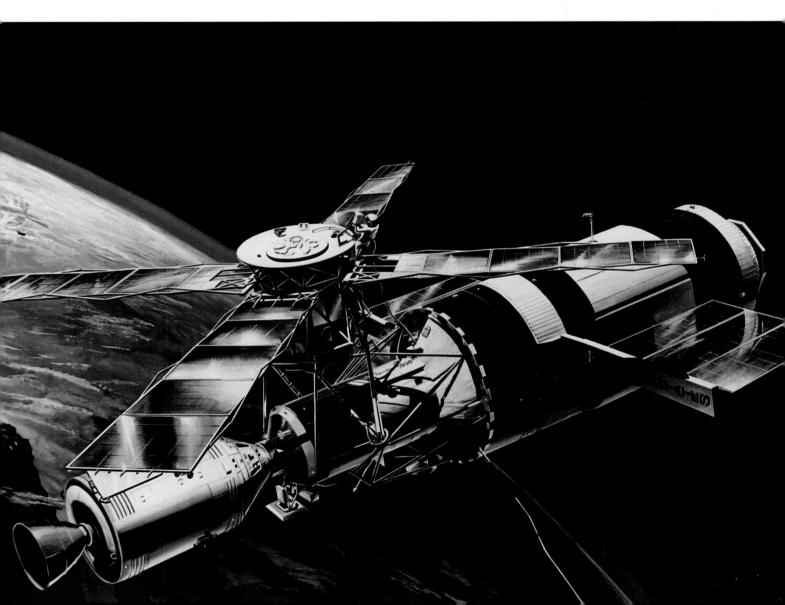

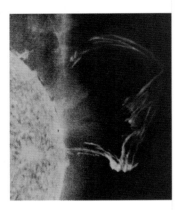

minutes of its launch, American tracking stations picked up signals showing fragments had dropped away from the rocket lifting it into orbit. Within three weeks of the launch, and before any crew could board the new station, it became clear that it was breaking up, and the experiment was abandoned.

Once again, the pace of the space race was speeding up quite dramatically. Before the Russians could launch their next space station, the Americans took center stage once again,

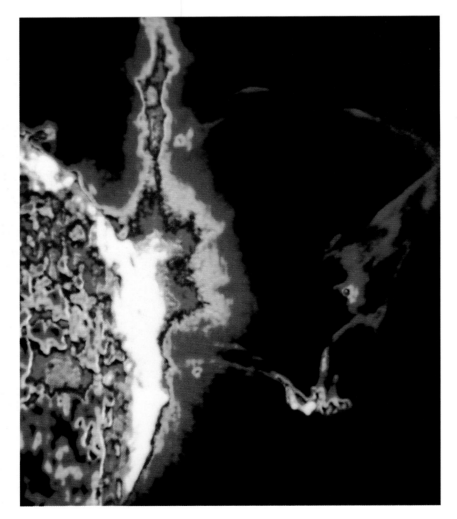

with the launch of Skylab on May 14, 1973, almost seven weeks after the unsuccessful launch of *Salyut 2*. The station itself was constructed, at minimum cost, from the fourth stage of a *Saturn 5* rocket, with the cylindrical liquid hydrogen tank converted into roomy accommodation on two levels for a crew of three. On the lower level was a wardroom with sleeping compartments, and the upper level contained a spacious workshop and laboratory with food and water storage.

Like the Salyuts, the Skylab was launched into orbit unmanned. The first crew of three was to follow later aboard an Apollo command and service module combination. However, it soon became clear that the station had encountered problems. Just over a minute after launch, air pressure had torn away the large protective shield that deflected sunlight and small meteorites from the large window of the workshop, together with one of the two banks of solar panels intended to provide power for the station.

Ironically, the four solar panel arrays that generated power for the Apollo telescope mount, an instrument for carrying out solar observations, had deployed perfectly. The situation was serious because, without the shield, the internal temperature of the station would rise too high and the power supplies would fall too low. In order to save the project, Mission Control had to steer Skylab into an altitude that partly shaded its interior from overheating while keeping the ATM solar arrays in a position where they could generate enough power to keep the station functioning.

When astronauts Charles "Pete" Conrad, Joseph Kerwin, and Paul Weitz were launched into orbit on May 25, 1973, they took more than seven hours to rendezvous with Skylab, and then carried out a careful reconnaissance to check the damage. Not only was one solar array missing altogether, but its twin had been prevented from deploying by a fragment of the broken shield. To add to their problems, when they tried to dock with Skylab, there were malfunctions in the docking system.

THIS PAGE

Top A huge solar eruption seen in this enlarged Spectroheliogram obtained during the *Skylab 3* mission that took place from July to September, 1973. *Above* A color density rendition of the solar eruption taken from *Skylab 3* in 1973.

OPPOSITE PAGE

This spectacular photograph of the Sun's solar flares was taken on December 19, 1973, during the third and final manned Skylab mission.

One by one the problems were solved. They made modifications to the docking system switches so they were able to join their spacecraft to the Skylab entry port. They climbed aboard the space station wearing breathing apparatus in case of poisonous fumes from the overheated furnishings and equipment in the workshop, but all was well, except that it was too warm to sleep aboard the station. Instead, they slept in the cramped surroundings of the multiple docking adapter, a cylindrical space between the Apollo command module and Skylab proper, which had its own heat shield.

To remedy the situation, they put on space suits and climbed out through an air lock to deploy a makeshift sunshade, causing the internal temperature to fall and make the station habitable. Two weeks after arriving on board they finally succeeded in cutting away the obstruction and allowing the remaining solar array to deploy properly and charge the station's storage batteries. Finally, during the remaining part of their four-week stay in space, they took pictures of Earth's surface and of solar activity, and carried out a series of biomedical experiments to monitor the effects of weightlessness.

The first crew returned on June 22, 1973, with the second crew being launched on July 28. After docking, the crew found their spacecraft's maneuvering engines were leaking fuel, and Mission Control prepared to send a second Apollo craft to rescue the astronauts. Fortunately, the leaks were less severe than they first appeared, and the mission was completed on schedule, after a total of fifty-nine days aboard the station.

The third and final crew reached the station on November 16, 1973, and stayed in space for a total of twelve weeks, during which time the effects of weightlessness, reinforced by a strict exercise program, caused each crew member to grow in height by an inch or more as their spines stretched in the absence of gravity. When they returned to Earth in February 1974, there were no further Skylab

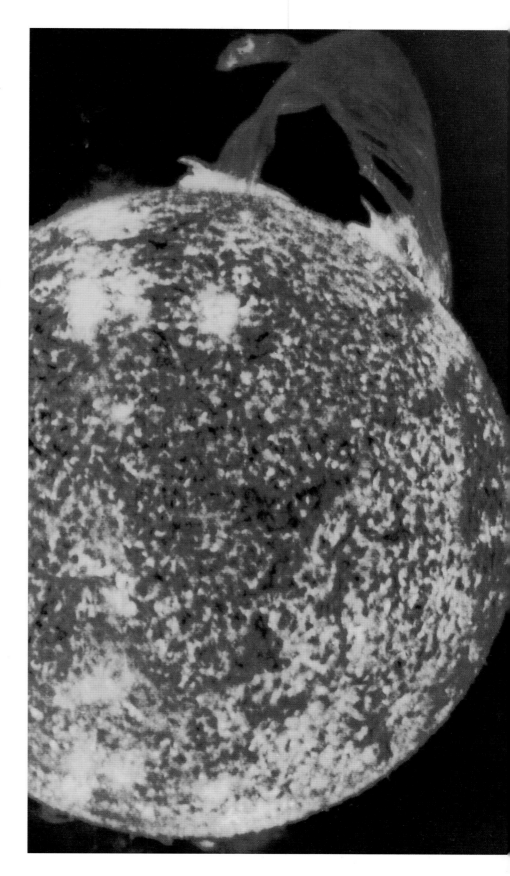

The Russians embarked on their most ambitious space station program with the launching of the core module of the Mir station on February 20, 1986. This had no fewer than six docking ports, for specialized living and working modules to be attached to it, in addition to regular resupply and crew replacement craft.

In March 1987, the Kvant 1 astrophysics laboratory almost doubled the size of the station. Kvant 2 was added in February 1990, with washing facilities and an air lock for work outside the station, and Kristall, which followed a month later, providing an additional docking port and more laboratory space. The Spektr module of March 1995 carried additional solar arrays and scientific equipment and was followed by the Priroda module in April 1996, with still more sensors and scanners.

The complete station weighs 130 tons, and has been used for twenty-nine Soyuz flights and eight flights by the space shuttle, carrying around 100 different astronauts over its thirteen years in space. It burst into prominence on June 25, 1997, when an unmanned Progress supply vessel collided with the Spektr module while using a new guidance system for docking. The module lost pressure and electrical power, and the astronauts had to evacuate it and seal it off from the rest of the station.

Unfortunately, all the hatches that would have needed to be closed to seal off any damaged section of the station had now been partially blocked by supply tubes and electrical cables. NASA astronaut James Foale struggled to disconnect the mass of connections from preventing the hatch of the Soyuz escape capsule being closed, if they had to abandon

Right The crew of the space shuttle *Atlantis* took this picture of Russia's Mir space station over Australia on March 23, 1996.

the station. Meanwhile Russian cosmonaut Sasha Lazutkin, who saw the supply vessel hit the Spektr module, knew where the leak was. He started furiously disconnecting the cable connections in the hatchway leading to the damaged module in an effort to save the rest of the station rather than abandon it.

Unfortunately, the last cable was a power cable, and it showered the crew with sparks when they began cutting it. Lazutkin had to enter the Spektr module to find the plug that would allow him to disconnect the final cable. Unfortunately, as part of the emergency drill is to open the valves on the station's spare oxygen tanks to boost the internal pressure, there was now a positive pressure on the wrong side of the hatch. To make matters worse, the facing of the hatch was smooth and offered no positive grip. With options rapidly

running out, Lazutkin remembered that there were spare hatch lids strapped to the walls of the station. Quickly they cut the straps and placed it in position, looking for the hooks normally needed to hold it in place. This time, the drop in pressure inside the Spektr module worked in their favor, and the pressure differential locked the lid firmly in place saving both the crew and the station.

In all, Mir survived a total of 1,600 breakdowns, and 16,500 different scientific experiments were carried out on board, by the time the last crew of two Russians and a Frenchman left the station on August 27, 1999. Its future remains uncertain, with experts predicting a loss of altitude and a final plunge to Earth early in the year 2000, unless the Russians raise the finance for it to be boosted into a higher and safer orbit.

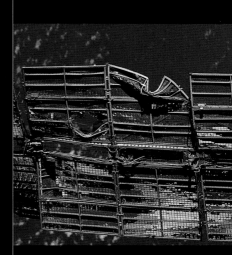

Above A close-up view of the solar array panel on Mir, shows damage incurred by the impact of a Russian unmanned Progress resupply ship.
Left The damage done to the solar array panel is clearly shown on this view of Mir.

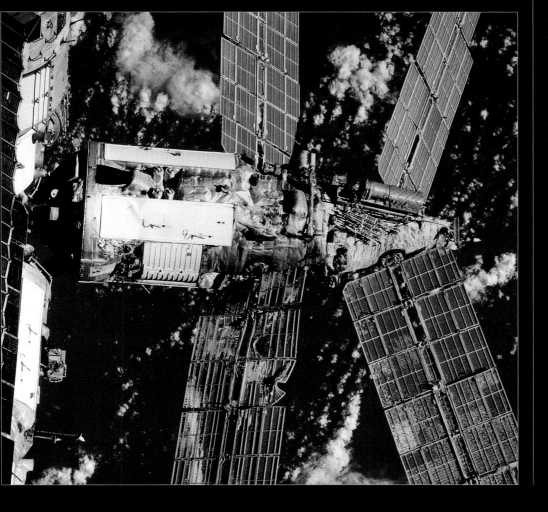

missions planned. Instead, a space shuttle mission to the station would be mounted in the early 1980s to attach a powered module that could then be used to boost it into a higher and safer orbit.

These plans were dashed by increased sunspot activity in 1978 and 1979, which caused Earth's atmosphere to expand to the point where it exerted additional drag on the empty station. By April 1979, it was clear that Skylab would fall to Earth within a matter of weeks. All that could be done was to change its attitude, and so increase or decrease the drag, to bring the station down in the Indian Ocean, though trails of fragments were also picked up across a remote part of the Australian bush.

After Skylab's demise, it was the Russians' turn to forge ahead. Even though Skylab had been a relatively low-cost development that had proved surprisingly successful, the fact that it had been launched as a complete craft was something of a dead end in the development of larger and bigger stations. Instead, the Russians

OPPOSITE PAGE
Launch of the Soviet *Soyuz 13* on December 18, 1973.

THIS PAGE
Above V. Bykovsky and S. Jaehn pictured inscribing their autographs on the sides of the landing ship of the Soyuz program on September 3, 1978.
Right The carrier rocket with the spacecraft Soyuz, designed by S.P. Korolyov, on show in Baikonur, Russia, January 1987.

put a great deal of effort into developing automatic docking systems and multiple docking ports to allow space stations to be extended and resupplied for long periods.

Salyut 3 had been launched on June 25, 1974, and eight days later two cosmonauts were sent up, this time wearing space suits in case of depressurization problems. They remained on board for just over two weeks before returning to Earth, but problems still occurred. The next crew found it difficult to rendezvous with the space station and used up too much fuel trying to dock with it. They returned to Earth, and the station was left unmanned until it was deliberately burned up in the atmosphere on January 24, 1975.

Salyut 4 suffered similar problems after its launch in December, 1974. The first crew boarded the craft successfully and stayed for a month. The second crew ran into problems on the ascent, when the second stage of the rocket failed to separate. Though this was corrected from the ground, the additional drag forced them to return to the surface without ever reaching orbit. The third crew were more successful, staying aboard for two months, and again the craft was left unmanned after the three missions, before being brought down over the Pacific in February 1977.

The three missions for Salyut 5 followed a similar plot. The first was a success, although the crew was brought back to Earth ahead of schedule, landing at night. The second mission failed to rendezvous with the station, and again the crew had to return in darkness. The third mission was successful, but lasted a mere two weeks and four days.

At first, it seemed that Salyut 6, launched on September 29, 1977, was going to continue this discouraging tradition. The first cosmonauts to reach it were unable to dock with it, as the station's latching mechanism failed to operate. Though Salyut 6 had a docking port at either end, the crew had used up too much fuel and were forced to return to Earth. As a last attempt to rescue the project, space engineer Georgy Grechko was sent up in

another Soyuz, assisted by Yuri Romanenko, on December 11, 1977.

They reached the space station and docked successfully at the second port. They unloaded the repair equipment they had brought with them, entered Salyut 6, and prepared to examine the docking mechanism at the opposite end of the craft. In order to do this, Grechko had to climb out of the spacecraft, through an air lock, and work his way around the outside surface using a series of handholds to reach the docking port. Romanenko meanwhile also emerged from the air lock and waited to see if his help would be needed.

To his unbounded surprise, Grechko found the mechanism worked perfectly, and the problem must have been caused by a fault on their predecessors' Soyuz. He was relaxing and watching the awesome spectacle of Earth rotating far below him when he was horrified to see Romanenko had lost his footing and was drifting helplessly past him, out into space, almost beyond hope of rescue. Grechko stretched out to the limit of his reach, and just managed to grasp the end of his comrade's disconnected lifeline. Carefully he pulled him back, and they climbed back through the air lock, only to find to their alarm that the instruments were reporting a major air leak.

This could have been fatal as there was no way of reaching their Soyuz capsule except by going through the airlock into the space station, and then through the docking hatches. Fortunately, it proved to be another instrumentation fault, and from that point onward all went according to plan. Grechko and Romanenko stayed in orbit for more than three months, during which they were resupplied by a robot spacecraft that locked itself automatically to the other docking port. When their mission was over they were replaced by a whole succession of changeover crews, and by 1982 missions were lasting more than six months at a time. The space station concept, it appeared, was here to stay.

LIVING IN ZERO GRAVITY

As space stations made it possible for astronauts to live for much longer periods in weightless conditions, designers took greater care to keep them comfortable. Aboard Skylab, each crew member slept in a vertical sleeping bag and had the use of a shower and toilet compartment specially designed to function in zero-gravity. After washing or showering, floating droplets of water had to be drawn off using a hosepipe with a suction head. Foods were chosen for variety and ease of eating, and the station was provided with heating and cooling equipment. Aboard Mir, astronauts preferred to have one surface of the operations area designated as the floor, in spite of the lack of gravity. This was covered in dark green carpet, with light green colored walls, and a ceiling lit with fluorescent lamps, while the living area was painted in soft pastel shades to aid relaxation.

Both American and Russian astronauts experienced problems with adjusting to weightless conditions. On Earth, gravity causes blood and other body fluids to flow

Below **Oranges and grapefruit brought from Earth get a popular reception by the Mir-22 crew members.**

downward to the legs, from which they are pumped upward by the heart. Without gravity, these bodily fluids flowed into the upper parts of the body depressing the appetite, so that the astronauts tended to eat little, but often. To alleviate these effects, Skylab carried an exercise bicycle and a negative pressure chamber which expanded the body's lower blood vessels to maintain circulation. The Russians used a treadmill for exercise, and an ingenious spring-loaded sweatshirt to exercise the upper body muscles while running.

Below Dafydd R. Williams from the Canadian Space Agency completes a "run" in the Lower Body Negative Pressure device onboard the Spacelab Science Module in 1998.

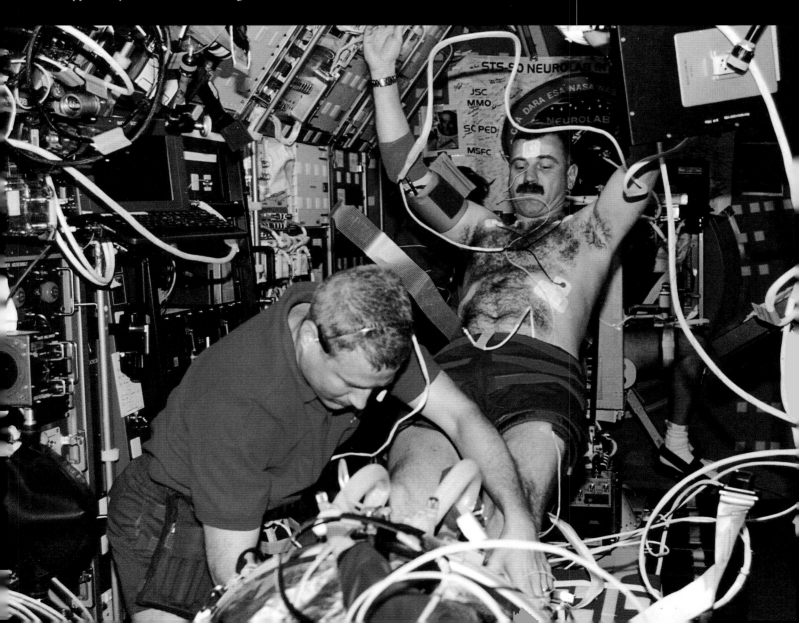

TO THE SOLAR SYSTEM AND BEYOND: UNMANNED PROBES

To the Moon, Mars, Venus, and Mercury—unmanned probes can reach far beyond the range of human astronauts. See how they worked, when they were launched, and what they were sent to find out.

Almost from its beginnings, space exploration has been pulled in two different directions. The spectacle of astronauts standing on the surface of the Moon, carrying out complex maintenance work against the stupendous panorama of Earth, or on space walks aboard orbiting spacecraft, are the most enduring images of the Space Age. Yet the undeniable limitations of manned space ventures are the costs and the complexity of the technology involved. For the enormous budgets that made it possible for Neil Armstrong to take his "one giant leap for mankind" and return to his home planet, a whole series of unmanned probes could have been sent to more distant destinations, still far beyond the range of human astronauts.

The first spacecraft of all were too small and too simple to carry human crews. But with astonishing speed, the targets of the robot spacecraft became much more ambitious. On January 2, 1959, the Russians launched a probe called *Luna 1*. This was carried on the same type of rocket used for the early Sputnik Earth satellites, but fitted with an additional booster stage to carry the 800 pound (363 kilogram) craft beyond the reach of Earth's gravity.

The power carried *Luna 1* into space, but the problem was in the navigation. Instead of flying close to the Moon, or even impacting on the lunar surface, the spacecraft missed its target by 3,700 miles (5,953 kilometers), and eventually took up an orbit around the Sun. Nevertheless, it sent back information on solar

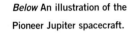

Below An illustration of the Pioneer Jupiter spacecraft.

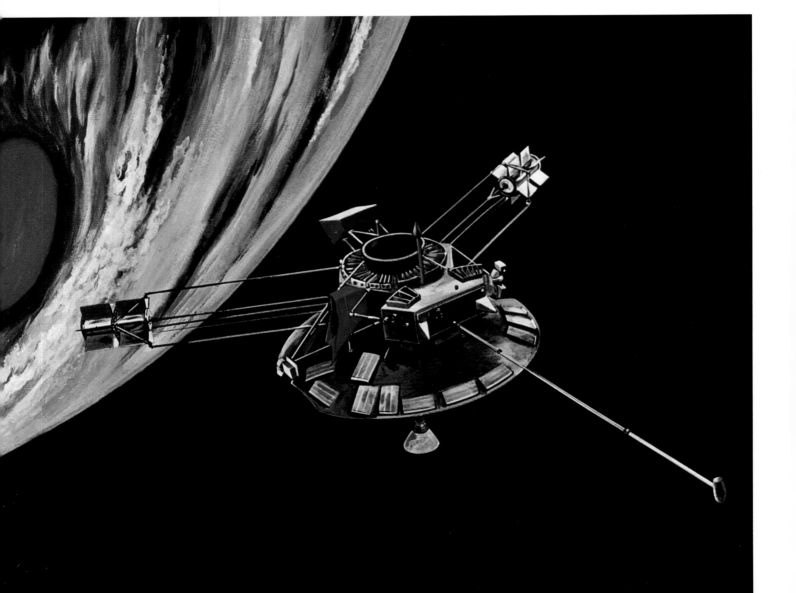

and cosmic radiation, and allowed observers on the ground to measure the density of matter in interstellar space. Meanwhile, the pace of development was speeding up. *Luna 2*, launched in September 1959, did score a direct hit on the Moon, on the eastern fringe of the Sea of Serenity.

For the time being, the United States space program was lagging behind its Soviet counterpart. The first three Pioneer space probes failed to complete more than a fraction of their journeys. *Pioneer 4* followed *Luna 1* in missing the Moon by more than twice its designed separation of 15,000 miles (24,000 kilometers) before it too went into orbit around the Sun. Before improved versions could be built and launched, the Russians produced another spectacular coup. Their *Luna 3*, launched on October 4, 1959, two years to the day after *Sputnik 1* not only approached close enough to the Moon to swing around behind it before returning to its home planet, but it was able to photograph almost three-quarters of the side of the Moon hidden from Earth observation, from an altitude of 4,900 miles (7,880 kilometers).

The next stage in the development of lunar probes meant developing a control system that could brake the craft to a soft and survivable landing. Because of the absence of any atmosphere, the only way of slowing the craft was to use a retro-rocket engine, which called for very precise navigation and very sensitive control of the rocket thrust. The American *Ranger 3* probe showed the difficulties of achieving this when, in January 1962, the retro-engine delivered too much power and prevented the craft from landing, sending it soaring away from the lunar surface and eventually into orbit around the Sun!

The remainder of the Ranger series of spacecraft were programmed to send pictures back to Earth, showing views of the lunar surface right up to the moment of impact, which was still too much of a shock for the craft to survive in a working condition. Once again it fell to the Russians to make the first successful soft landing on another planet, with their second series of Luna spacecraft. These weighed just under two tons, and were designed to land a 220 pound (100 kilogram) instrument package on the lunar surface, softly enough to function after the moment of impact.

At first the spacecraft was sent into Earth orbit. After a single complete circuit, the final stage rocket was fired to head the spacecraft on course for the Moon. When, within 46 miles (74 kilometers) of its target, the radar and

Above The Surveyor space craft.
Below left An illustration of the Surveyor probe touching down.

TOURING THE FURTHER REACHES

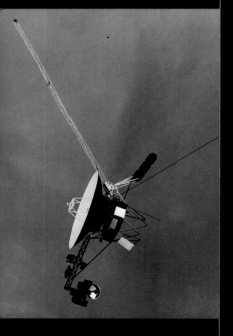

The precise navigation techniques developed to steer *Mariner 10*, past both Venus and Mercury were used on a much more ambitious scale, to enable two U.S. space probes to visit most of the remaining planets of the solar system, in a single voyage. *Pioneer 10*, launched in 1972 on its way to Jupiter, the largest of the planets, was able to send back more than 300 pictures of Jupiter and its satellites, before heading past Pluto on its way into deep space. Among them were images of the Great Red Spot, a huge atmospheric storm first observed by astronomers more than three centuries ago. It was followed by *Pioneer 11*, which was accelerated by Jupiter's gravity onto a trajectory for Saturn. Its journey took six years, at the end of which it passed within 21,000 miles (33,790 kilometers) of Saturn's ring system, before it too headed for the depths of space.

The Pioneers were succeeded by the larger and more sophisticated *Voyager 1* and *Voyager 2* spacecraft. These were launched in the early autumn of 1977 and reached Jupiter two years later. Both craft sent back high-quality pictures of the storms that racked the bands of cloud covering Jupiter, and of the four largest of Jupiter's total of sixteen moons. Just over a year later, both Voyager flew past Saturn, revealing a total of seven different rings of ice particles around the planet, together with a total of no less than twenty-two moons, the smallest of which are only a few miles across.

Voyager 2 was then boosted onto a new trajectory to take it past Uranus, which it reached nine years after launching. Out there, in the darkest and coldest reaches of the solar system, the planet appeared as a smooth, cloud-covered sphere, banded by eleven rings and circled by fifteen satellites. Finally, the spacecraft reached Neptune, after twelve years of traveling through space, revealing it as a cloud-covered planet with a faint ring system, eight moons, and an atmosphere of hydrogen, helium, and methane. Its surface showed a dark spot, in a similar location to the Great Red Spot of Jupiter, surrounded by clouds of frozen methane, but traveling across the surface at more than 1,200 miles an hour (1,930 kilometers an hour).

Both Voyager craft like their Pioneer predecessors, are heading out into deep space on very different trajectories. *Pioneer 10* will reach the vicinity of the star Aldebaran, but its journey will take eight million years. *Voyager 2* is heading for the star Sirius, which it will pass in a comparatively trifling 358,000 years. All the probes will long since have ceased to radiate signals, though NASA scientists are hopeful they can continue extracting information, from the Voyagers in particular, for the next thirty years.

Not all unmanned space probes have been sent to inspect our planetary neighbors. In 1986, the return of Halley's comet triggered a series of probes launched by Russia, Japan, and the European Space Agency, to examine the structure and composition of this rare visitor. The Japanese Sakigake and Suisei probes passed through the shock waves that the comet's passage through space creates, ahead of its nucleus, while the Russian probes *Vega 1* and *Vega 2* followed a trajectory that would take them within 5,600 miles (9,000 kilometers) of the comet's nucleus.

Closest of all was the European Space Agency's Giotto spacecraft, which approached to within a mere 375 miles (603 kilometers) of the comet's nucleus. In the process it sustained a constant battering from fragments of the material making up the comet, which damaged its camera but left other sensors functioning. The information generated by all these probes showed that the comet was made up of a dark, dumb-bell shaped nucleus only a few miles across, but weighing 100 billion tons, and which ejected jets of water and carbon monoxide and dust in its wake, as it traced its brilliant arc across the darkness of space.

OPPOSITE PAGE

A scientist works on the
Mariner 2 probe.

THIS PAGE

Below left Mariner 5 on its
mission to Venus.
Below right The Viking probe
before takeoff.

navigation equipment that had brought the
Luna probe this far was dropped to reduce the
landing weight. The retro-rocket engine then
burned to reduce the descent speed. Finally, a
hinged arm projecting downward from the
bottom of the spacecraft then activated a
circuit, when it touched the surface, causing
the spherical instrument package at the top of
the probe to be thrown clear. It was designed
to lose energy by bouncing across the surface
like a ball, while its heavily weighted base
caused it to stop the right way up, to deploy its
camera and antennae.

Even so, it took a long time for the
equipment to work properly. A total of eight
probes were launched between 1963 and
1965, before *Luna 9* finally succeeded in early
1966. For the first time, pictures were sent
back to Earth from the surface of the Moon,
over the four days of operation before the
probe's batteries ran down.

The Americans, once again running close
behind, ran into similar difficulties. Their
Surveyor probes were designed to achieve a
soft landing on broadly similar principles. Half
an hour before the planned touchdown time,
the craft was to be turned to angle its retro-
rocket engine vertically downward. A special
altitude measuring radar was used to ignite the

retro-rocket, which also caused the radar to be
ejected from the rocket nozzle. The retro-
rocket was backed up by a set of vernier retro
motors that came into operation 52 miles
(84 kilometers) above the surface.

The retro-rocket engine was designed to
burn out, and separate from the spacecraft at
37,000 feet (11,300 meters) above the surface,
with the remainder of the descent being
controlled by the vernier motors. These would
finally cut off at 14 feet (4.3 meters) from the
surface, with the craft then falling at just
3.5 miles per hour (5.6 kilometers per hour).
The motors would then cut off to avoid too
much disturbance of the surface, and the final
fall would be absorbed by shock absorbing
landing pads.

Although the first Explorer was launched a
full four months after *Luna 9*, it hit its target
first time. The descent engine and the vernier
motors all operated as planned, and the probe
made a successful soft landing. Over a six week
period, including a shutdown of two weeks
during the lunar night, a total of more than
11,000 pictures was transmitted back to Earth.
Although two later Surveyors were lost when
different parts of the retro engine system failed
to fire, others sent back thousands more
pictures and data of the density and

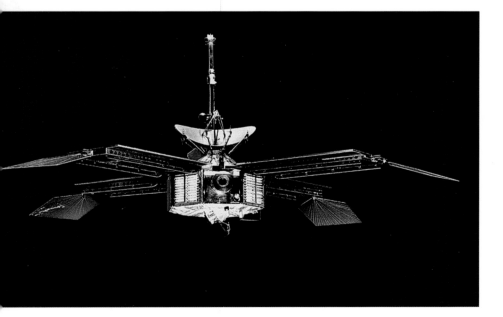

composition of the lunar surface. Once the technology for delivering soft landings had been developed, both the Americans and the Russians sent a whole series of progressively more ambitious probes to the Moon. In September 1970, the Russian *Luna 16* soft landed in an area called the Sea of Fertility, and ground control issued a series of signals which commanded it to lower a soil sampling drilling rig, which bored into the surface and lifted a core sample to be stored in a spherical chamber at the top of the spacecraft. After twenty-six hours on the Moon, an ascent rocket was fired which sent the upper section of the spacecraft on a trajectory back to Earth, carrying the soil sample with it, while the lower section remained on the Moon, in order to measure temperature and radiation levels and send the data back down to ground control.

Two months later, the Russians achieved a still more remarkable coup. *Luna 17* made a soft landing on the Sea of Rains. This time the craft opened up to reveal a set of ramps, down which an eight-wheeled roving vehicle set off to explore the area. This first lunar rover, called *Lunokhod 1*, covered a distance of more than 6 miles (9.5 kilometers) in a period of more than ten months, testing soil samples and sending back video pictures. In January 1973, this was surpassed by *Lunokhod 2*, which covered more than 20 miles (32 kilometers) in the area of the Sea of Serenity, under commands from ground controllers.

Beyond the Moon, the engineers developing the space probes next turned their attention to the Sun. *Pioneer 5*, the first truly interplanetary probe, was launched on March 11, 1960, followed in 1965 by a series of later Pioneer probes that were established in orbits around the Sun, at both greater and lesser distances than that of Earth, to monitor factors like the solar wind and its effects on Earth's magnetic field. Meanwhile, the Russians had turned their attention to the mysteries of the planet Venus, and launched two abortive probes in early 1961.

Above An artist's concept of the Viking lander as it heads for touch down on Mars.
Above right The Viking lander is shown in an illustration on the surface of Mars.

Only with the arrival of *Venera 3* on October 18, 1967 did any worthwhile information filter back from this mysterious planet. The probe reported atmospheric temperatures of more than 518 degrees Fahrenheit and pressures twenty times higher than those on the surface of Earth, before the transmitter failed still 15 miles (24 kilometers) above the surface. Conditions at ground level were finally revealed by *Venera 7*, which survived for fifteen minutes at a surface temperature of 891 degrees Fahrenheit, sufficient to melt lead, and a pressure of ninety atmospheres.

Two more Russian probes, *Venera 9* and *10*, were put into orbit around the planet in the summer of 1975, and each one released a soft-lander probe that carried video cameras. The spherical lander was specially designed to spend as little time descending, through the fiercely hot atmosphere, as possible, thanks to a parachute that released it into free fall while still 30 miles (48 kilometers) above the surface. Both landers sent back pictures of the barren stony surface. Later probes confirmed an atmosphere consisting mainly of carbon dioxide, clouds that produced sulphuric acid rain, which boiled before it reached the planet's surface, and endless violent thunderstorms. Subsequent American probes brought back more detailed information on the atmosphere of Venus and showed that its

shape is more perfectly spherical than Earth, with generally flatter surface contours.

Earth's other near neighbor, Mars, has proved an easier objective for robot explorers. The American probe *Mariner 4*, flew past the planet on July 14, 1965, at a range of 6,000 miles (9,650 kilometers), and transmitted data showing the Martian atmosphere exerted only 0.01 atmospheres at the surface of the planet, which was covered in impact craters very similar to those on the Moon. Because the distance separating Mars from Earth varies due to Mars's more elliptical orbit, NASA was able to send a much heavier and more complex spacecraft in 1971, when this distance approached its minimum.

Mariner 9 was established in orbit around Mars at a time when a vast dust storm was raging on the planet, so large that it could be made out through powerful telescopes from Earth. Once the dust settled, the probe sent back more than 7,000 video pictures showing a series of enormous dormant volcanoes, and a huge deep rift valley, the Valles Marinaris, extending one-fifth of the way around the planet's surface. In addition, networks of what appear to be long dried-up watercourses hint at a past when the planet possessed moisture in abundance.

This achievement was surpassed by the American probes *Viking 1* and *2*, launched in August and September, 1975. *Viking 1* arrived first and established itself in orbit around Mars, sending back video pictures of possible landing sites for the robot probe it carried. Mission Control staff were able to maneuver the spacecraft to find an ideal site, and then to command the release of the lander vehicle over an area called Chryse Planitia. The lander's retro-rocket was fired to cause it to fall out of orbit, and after it entered the Martian atmosphere, a parachute opened at 19,000 feet (5,790 kilometers) to slow down the craft to a speed of 145 miles per hour (230 kilometers per hour). When 4,600 feet (1,400 meters) above the surface, the parachute was released, and the rocket engine used to slow it down to a descent speed of 6 miles per hour (9.5 kilometers per hour), by the time of touchdown.

Viking 1's lander touched down on July 20, 1976, followed by *Viking 2's* lander, which reached the surface in a region called Utopia Planitia, on September 3. Both craft carried soil scoops and an onboard analysis laboratory to probe for any signs of life on the planet's surface. Despite the spectacular achievement of these entirely unmanned spacecraft that continued to send back information into the early 1980s, the signs were promising but inconclusive, and so the search continues, using ever more clever unmanned craft to extend the search further and further.

Unmanned spacecraft were the first man-made artefacts to be launched into space, and continue to form the basis of current space research, thanks to spin-offs from programs such as Skylab and Apollo. Robot explorers cannot only achieve soft landings in dauntingly harsh and distant conditions, but the sophisticated navigational and control systems that carried astronauts to the Moon and back have also steered cleverly-designed probes across the furthest reaches of the solar system. Even where funds may be restricted for more ambitious developments, the launching of future probes will maintain the vigil on space through the window first opened by *Sputnik 1* more than forty years ago.

Hitching a ride to Mercury

Mariner 10, the American space probe launched in November 1973, had a double purpose. After successfully flying past Venus and sending back the first video pictures of the planet, it followed a trajectory that used the gravity of Venus to alter the course of the probe and slow it down so that it would perform a series of flybys over the innermost planet of the solar system, Mercury. This technique would eventually make it possible for probes to visit most of the outermost planets of the solar system on a single voyage, but in this case, *Mariner 10* made three sweeps past the planet at approximately six-month intervals.

It revealed an even more unwelcoming world than either Mars or Venus. The atmosphere contains traces of argon, neon, and helium, at a pressure one-trillionth that of Earth. The barren surface is covered with impact craters, and its temperature varies between 210 degrees Fahrenheit below zero at night, and a peak of 940 degrees Fahrenheit under the fierce glow of the Sun, which, at its closest approach, is a mere 28 million miles (45 million kilometers), compared with the 93 million miles (150 million kilometers) separating Earth from the Sun.

Above Mariner 10 view of Mercury.

SPIN·OFFS
FROM SPACE

Computers, microchips, freeze-dried food, satellite communications, weather study and prediction, orbital telescopes, virtual reality programs, and electric vehicles are just some of the successful products resulting from the space program.

OPPOSITE PAGE
The Wind spacecraft, part of the global Geospace Science Initiative to measure properties of the solar wind before it reaches earth.

THIS PAGE
A Mars art concept of possible exploration programs showing the updated Pathfinder rover.

From the very beginning of space exploration, most people have tended to view it as an exceedingly expensive luxury, affordable only by the superpowers, and only justifiable by them at times when questions of global prestige, between the competing systems of capitalism and communism, were involved. Once the ultimate goal of placing humans on the surface of the Moon was achieved, public interest tended to wane, and even the most spectacular achievements of robot probes and landers, and the missions of the space shuttle, failed to disturb a growing public apathy over the future of space research.

In the case of the Russians, the breakup of the Soviet Union, and the country's crippling economic problems, put the brakes on future space programs in a way that would have seemed inconceivable in the 1980s. Similarly, the withdrawal of one of the two contestants in the East-West space race eliminated the urgency from the competition and from the political agenda of the United States. NASA had to find new reasons for the work it was doing to insure that the funds were made available for that work to continue.

Nevertheless, public apathy over the value of space exploration is matched by a lack of information over the resulting benefits. The huge sums needed to fund the Apollo technology were essential when human lives were at stake. Blasting astronauts across the hostile gulfs of space to touch down on an airless, waterless world where their survival times would have been measured in minutes if anything had gone wrong was a highly dangerous enterprise. It could only have been carried through with the kind of attention to detail and refusal to compromise, on the grounds of cost, that would have been impossible in any other technological enterprise.

This suggests a permanent imbalance in the economics of space research, on the lines of huge amounts of money spent bringing a little knowledge in return. The truth is really a great deal more encouraging. NASA points out that the current space program accounts for less than 1 percent of the American budget, and that on average every dollar spent on the space program results in seven dollars paid back into the economy, from increased jobs and economic growth. But the biggest benefit of all is impossible to quantify. The list of spin-offs from space technology into people's daily lives is enormous, varied, and still growing.

The development of rescue blankets made from recycled plastic milk bottles that can keep people warm, even when wet, was developed from NASA's research into lightweight metal insulation for spacecraft, and is one of the latest additions to the list. Another is the CCD chip technology used in the Hubble space telescope that is also being used in a device for imaging breast tissue more clearly so that it can detect the minute differences between benign and malignant tumors, and, avoid the need for a surgical biopsy of potential sufferers.

Smaller and more powerful computers were needed to make the moon program feasible in the first place, and the need to pack as much computing power into packages as light and compact as possible provided the incentive for the development of the microchip. This incorporated all the separate elements of an electrical circuit such as resistors, capacitors, and transistors into a single, precisely engineered wafer of semi-conductor material, with the added benefits of lower costs and higher speed of manufacture and reliability in operation.

More recently, space technology has produced the memory cube, a three-dimensional semiconductor package that has dozens of integrated circuits stacked on top of one another for still greater compactness and operating speed. Other advances that owe their origins to space developments include virtual reality (VR) systems, advanced keyboards, and lightweight compact disc systems.

Sometimes the links are less straightforward. NASA research into food suitable for long periods in space led to the development of a vegetable oil substitute based on microalgae. Because this contains two fatty acids found in human milk, though missing from most baby formulas, it can be used in the development of enriched baby foods. In a similar way, the technology developed to sterilize water for long periods in space is now being used to purify swimming pools, without chemicals. Passing a current through silver-copper alloy electrodes generates silver and copper ions that are toxic to algae and bacteria.

The thermoelectric technology used to cool spacecraft has also made it possible to deliver large amounts of heating or cooling capability from low-power sources, such as car cigarette lighter sockets. Plug-in accessories can heat water to 125 degrees Fahrenheit or provide the cooling power of a 10 pound (4.5 kilogram) block of ice. The environmental control system developed for the space shuttle has also been used to produce the Barorator, a device that monitors changes in atmospheric pressure and calculates the instantaneous rate of change as an aid to forecasting the weather. Aerodynamics research for spacecraft has also resulted in the production of a new design of golf ball with 500 surface dimples arranged in a pattern of 60 spherical triangles that maintains its initial velocity for longer reach and has a more stable flight path for even greater accuracy.

Other examples of successful spin-offs from space technology include personal alarms, emergency rescue cutters, storm warning systems, and better brakes and tires. Electric vehicles are using NASA's flywheel energy storage system, and corporate jet aircraft are flying with more efficient wing sections using NASA computer programs. Space technology has even extended into such everyday articles as wheelchairs, school buses, home security systems, sun and ski goggles, golf clubs, sports bras, batteries, and television screens. As space exploration proceeds, this unseen, and largely uncelebrated benefit, becomes ever greater in scope, and wider in its successful applications.

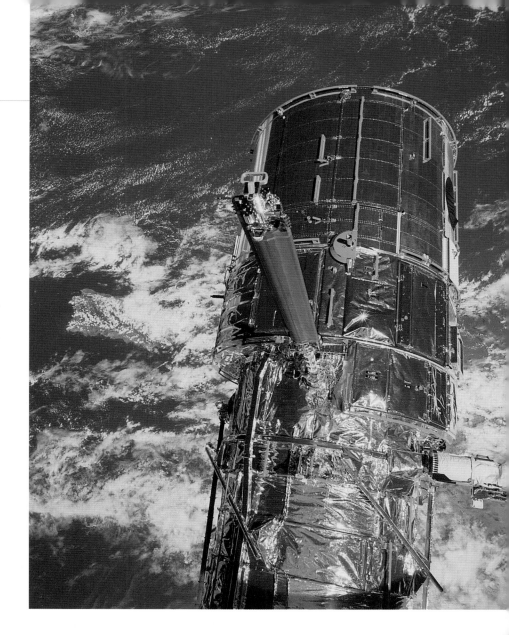

SPACE MEDICINE
AND THE WEIGHTLESS FACTORY

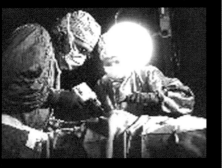

Medicine has become one of the most
successful fields for the application of space
technology. Potential sufferers from breast
cancer are routinely given X-ray examinations,
and the use of a solar cell sensor, positioned
directly below the X-ray film, allows the
system to be turned off automatically when
the film has been exposed to the optimum
amount of radiation to provide a clear picture.
This speeds up the process so that more
patients can be treated and the radiation
hazard for each one is greatly reduced.

NASA ultrasonics technology is
increasingly being used to assess the depth of
the damage suffered by burn victims. This
allows treatment to be matched more accurately
to the injuries involved. Image processing
techniques first developed for the space
program are now used to detect eye problems
in very young children, by sending light from

an electronic flash into the eye, and using a
photorefractor to analyze the retinal reflexes.

Robot technology has been used to
produce a patient-controlled wheelchair that
can respond to thirty-five one-word voice
commands, and modified space suit designs
have resulted in a cool suit used in the
treatment of multiple sclerosis, spina bifida,
cerebral palsy, and other related conditions.
Perhaps most dramatically of all, the sensor
and control systems used in satellites have
been harnessed to help patients suffering from
chronic pain or involuntary movement
disorders to use an implant device to manage
their conditions through electric stimulation
of specific nerve centers, or particular areas of
the brain.

The weightless conditions existing in
Earth orbit have made it possible to develop
industrial processes that can be carried out

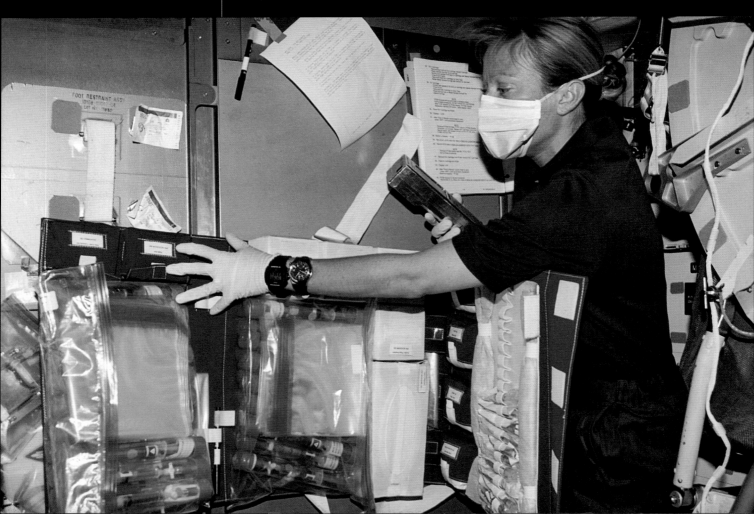

aboard space stations that can simply not be performed in ground-based factories. These include alloys like aluminum-lithium that will not mix properly under gravity, and other metallurgical operations, and the growing of better-quality crystals and semiconductor films than is currently possible in orthodox laboratories. Drugs have also been purified in space, using electrophoresis equipment specially designed to make the best use of the weightless conditions to produce greater yields and higher purity than is possible with earthbound equipment.

Other benefits include the use of space technology to make ground-based industrial processes, or machinery, more efficient. Magnetic bearings that were developed for the space shuttle are also used to support moving machinery without the need for direct physical contact. This avoids losses from friction, wear of the bearing surfaces, or the unwanted generation of heat. Current applications include electric power generation and the operation of machine tools. Microlasers used for cutting, drilling, or melting hard materials were originally developed for optical communications over interplanetary distances, and synthetic fluids that can be controlled by magnetic force have been able to cure persistent leakage problems in the making of semiconductor chips.

Even the production of spacecraft such as the shuttle has helped create technologies that have been used in other industries. The need for high-quality welds to insure the integrity of the external fuel tank produced a highly sophisticated automated laser welding system. This is able to track the surfaces of the two pieces of metal about to be welded, measuring any surface defects, gaps, and misfits and automatically adjusting the distance and height of the welding torch to take these factors into account. This is now being used in industry where similar levels of welding quality are needed.

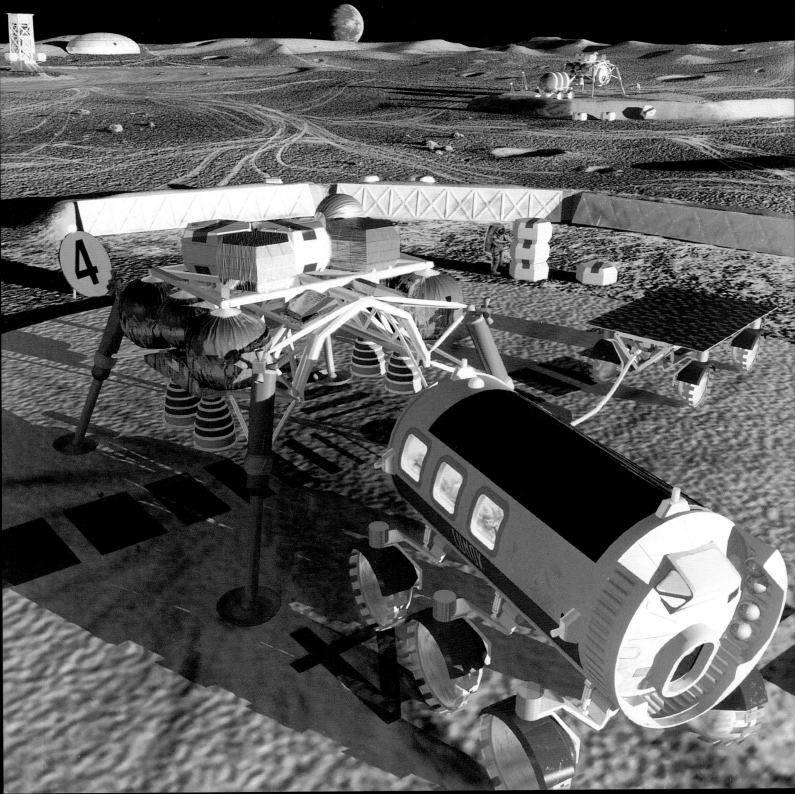

FUTURE PROSPECTS

Take a glimpse at what lies ahead in space exploration: colonies on the Moon, flights to Mars, deep space probes, and nuclear fusion rockets propelling us at stupendous speed into the deep and dark unknown.

OPPOSITE PAGE

An artist's concept of crews from Earth taking part in automated mining operations on the Moon.

THIS PAGE

This illustration shows a crew landing on Mars and using an unpressurized rover to unload cargo and supplies for their stay.

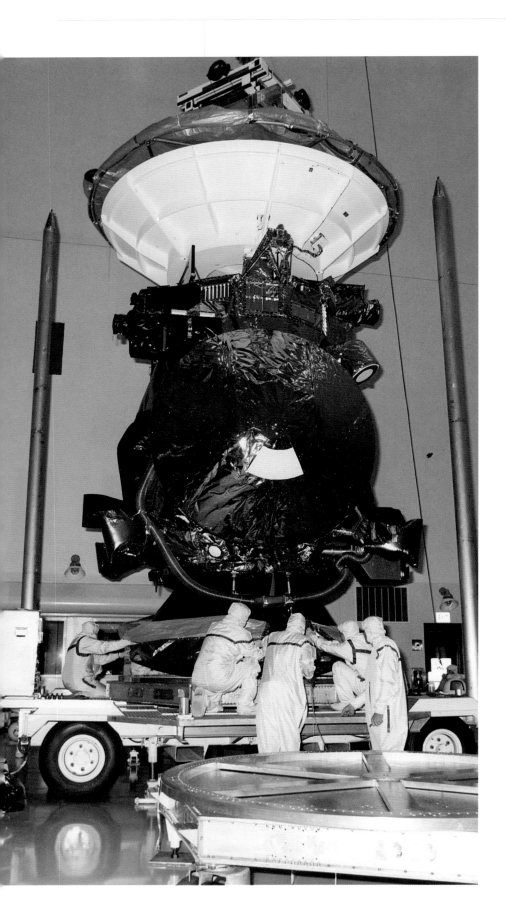

Left The Cassini spacecraft, which is scheduled to go on a four-year closeup mission to study the Saturnian system. *Above* An advanced artist's concept of the Near Earth Asteroid Rendezvous spacecraft rendezvousing with the asteroid Eros to send back data to Earth.

Following decades of stupendous achievements in space exploration, future priorities are less clear. With the breakup of the Soviet Union and the dramatic plunge in Russian financial resources, one of the main protagonists has virtually dropped out of the space race. While future projects will gain from international cooperation, there is little doubt that the pressure to beat the opposition to the next space milestone was a powerful inducement, both to the United States, and the Soviet governments, to find the backing needed for the next generation of space research. Fortunately, most of the technology needed to make it possible had already been developed.

In essence, there are four options. Future efforts may concentrate on more sophisticated satellites and space probes to tell us more about the solar system and the wider universe. The technology already exists for the building of more ambitious space stations to provide bases for valuable scientific research, and an investment for the future, in case funds become available for long-distance space travel. With present technology, it would be feasible to establish a long-term colony on the Moon, for a radical new view of the universe, and a source of the materials needed for life on Earth and for long-distance space flight. In addition, with straightforward developments of that technology, a mission to place human astronauts on the surface of Mars is within the bounds of possibility.

For all the expense and sophistication of the planetary probes launched over more than two decades, there are still sharp boundaries to the extent of our knowledge. Only one face of the planet Mercury has been filmed. There is still very little known of the surface of Venus, or of the polar regions of Mars, and the outermost planet Pluto still remains a mysterious distant object, with a single moon and an eccentric orbit that cuts across the path of Neptune at a sharp angle to the plane of the rest of the solar system.

The recent failure of NASA's Mars lander has caused despondency over the failure of its apparently reliable technology and has put a question mark over other similar systems. Probes that fly past their objectives tend to use quite different hardware, and the spacecraft intended to give the first clear view of Pluto will be smaller and more economical than any of its predecessors. Standing almost 4 feet (1 meter) tall and weighing some 350 pounds (159 kilograms), it will be controlled by an onboard computer that will navigate by the stars and be powered by a thermoelectric generator creating as much power as a domestic lightbulb.

The Pluto probe has one important deadline to meet. During the first years of this new century, the planet will be heading out away from the Sun, along its long and unusual orbit. In addition, Pluto and its moon will tend to cast deeper shadows on one another, reducing the opportunities for clear observation. An early launch would reach Pluto in around 2007, but the longer the probe is delayed the further it will have to travel and the longer it will take.

Apart from its unique objective, the Pluto mission will help set another important trend

in dramatically reducing the costs of making the spacecraft and sending it on its way. The intention is to limit each low-budget probe to a target ceiling of U.S.$150 million apiece. Within this limit, a series of ambitious probes will add to the information already gathered by their predecessors on Saturn and Jupiter, Venus, Uranus, and Neptune.

Already the first of these low-cost NASA probes is exploring the mysterious asteroid belt between the orbits of Mars and Jupiter. The NEAR (Near Earth Asteroid Rendezvous) probe, launched by a Delta rocket on February 17, 1996, is en route for the asteroid Eros, measuring approximately 15 miles by 9 miles by 9 miles (24 by 14.5 by 14.5 kilometers), and began orbiting the asteroid in February 2000.

Above This illustration shows a dirty snowball the size of a mountain ploughing through the solar system with the *Champollion* spacecraft anchoring to its surface to collect samples.

LOOKING FOR LIFE

One of the most exciting objectives of future space missions will be the search for extraterrestrial signs of life. Organic molecules have been found in fragments of meteorites, and the discovery of planetary systems around neighboring stars like Upsilon Andromeda that may include planets of a similar size, composition, and temperature to Earth, raise new possibilities that life may not be limited to our own planet.

Even within the solar system, new information on Callisto and Europa, satellites of Jupiter suggest that both moons have internal heat sources from a liquid center, together with reserves of carbon and water, both essential ingredients for the development of life.

In the shorter term, the most promising place to start the search for life on other planets is Mars. As long ago as 1988, the Soviet Union announced a plan for using eight Energiya rockets to lift enough material into Earth orbit that they would be able to assemble two nuclear-electric powered

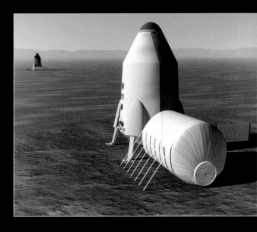

Left An illustration of a possible nuclear thermal transfer vehicle refuelling in a Mars-orbit near the Martian moon Phobos.
Above An artist's concept of a future outpost on Mars.

spaceships to be assembled free of Earth's gravity. Each of these ships would be able to make the journey to Mars, where they would begin to orbit the planet, allowing a pair of cosmonauts to descend to the surface aboard specially developed modules, that would also carry specially designed roving vehicles, with the second ship available for rescue or resupply. The main advantage of this approach is that the human visitors would be able to cover a much wider area in their search for life than even the most sophisticated automatic lander.

Another possible approach would involve landing on the Martian moon Phobos and establishing a scientific base on the satellite. This would begin with an unmanned vehicle being launched to carry the return vehicle and the expedition's equipment, and to maintain it in orbit around Mars. A month later a second ship carrying a crew of four astronauts would follow. They would dock with the first spacecraft and then allow two of the

astronauts to descend to the surface of Phobos, in order to set up the long-term monitoring experiments needed to watch for the requirements of life. Meanwhile the remaining two would carry out detailed examinations of the Martian surface, using remotely controlled roving vehicles sent down aboard automatic soft-landing probes.

These ambitious projects are theoretically possible using developments of current space technology. However, three main problems remain to be solved. The first is financial, since the sums needed would probably dwarf those involved in making possible the Apollo missions to the Moon. The other is biological, since the distances involved would mean the astronauts spending well over a year in zero-gravity conditions to cover the huge distances involved. The third is technological, since the different systems would have to function with a high level of reliability over longer distances and timescales with a minimum of maintenance.

Below This artwork imagines an exobiologist finding a porous relic of a hot spring, which could provide fossilized evidence of Martian life-forms.

Above A Geologist on a possible exploration on Mars.
Left An advanced artist's concept of a space station on Mars.

OPPOSITE PAGE

Top This concept illustrates a laser power station, perhaps drawing energy from the local environment, propelling a spacecraft throughout the solar system.

Bottom A possible lunar mining facility, complete with a marketing executive indicating the potential for a metal production plant.

THIS PAGE

The ice deposits on the Moon could help attenuate dangerous radiation on a solar-powered colony.

The mission began by flying past the asteroid Mathilde on June 27, 1997. The NEAR craft then flew past Earth before approaching Eros for the first time in December 1998. Unfortunately, a software problem delayed the burn of the craft's maneuvering engine, intended to place it in orbit around the asteroid on January 10, 1999. By the time it was solved the window of opportunity had closed. Instead, Mission Control let NEAR pass within 2,377 miles (2,829 kilometers) of the asteroid on December 23, before carrying out another burn on December 31 to establish the craft in orbit around the Sun, ready for another encounter with Eros on February 14, 2000.

The intention is to slow down the craft as it approaches the asteroid so it can be put into a series of progressively closer orbits, from a circular orbit at a distance of 122 miles (196 kilometers) down to an orbit of 22 miles (35 kilometers) above the surface. The spacecraft will remain in close orbit around the asteroid collecting detailed information

for the rest of the year, and at the end of that time it will be brought even closer to the asteroid's surface, with a possible soft landing attempt making use of the asteroid's relatively low gravity.

In the longer term, it may be possible to do more with the smaller asteroids than merely study them. Suggestions have been made for mining scarce and expensive raw materials that exist in abundance on these tiny masses of rock. These would depend on manned expeditions using existing shuttle technology to build a large expedition craft in Earth orbit. This could be sent to rendezvous with a suitable asteroid, for extracting metals like gold and platinum, using abundant solar energy to power the refining process, and extracting water for conversion into fuel for the return journey.

Space stations in orbit around Earth would dramatically reduce the cost of missions to and from the Moon, thanks to the use of space tugs, or reusable orbit transfer vehicles (OTVs), developed from specialized craft designed to enable technicians to maintain satellites in geostationary orbit. The amount of energy needed to travel between a space station and lunar orbit would be less than that required for docking with one of these specialized satellites.

This would make it possible to establish a base on the Moon for longer and more detailed lunar research. It would also be possible to establish a larger and more powerful space telescope, free of Earth's atmosphere, and more easily operated and maintained than when floating in Earth orbit. Radio telescopes could also be established on the far side of the Moon, where they would be shielded by the satellite's bulk from the vast amounts of radio noise generated by signals and broadcasts from terrestrial transmitters.

But the Moon also has powerful economic possibilities to make more ambitious spaceflights possible. The current search for water on the Moon would, if successful, open up the possibility of producing large quantities

of rocket fuel at a lunar base, together with the oxygen needed to create artificial atmospheres for a roomy and long-term lunar colony. NASA's estimates for the total construction cost of a lunar base, including living quarters, laboratories, and a power plant would be of a similar order to that spent on all the Apollo missions.

For the possibility of space travel beyond the solar system, some more powerful propellant would be needed to raise the speed of a spacecraft much higher than that of those craft developed for the Moon missions. Nuclear fission rockets have already been developed that use heat from a small on board reactor to heat hydrogen gas to a very high temperature before shooting it out of the rear of the rocket in order to propel the craft in the normal way. Because the resulting thrust is some 70 percent greater than the equivalent conventional rocket, and has a much greater endurance, the speed and range of a nuclear powered spacecraft would be much greater than the current generation of rocket-propelled space vehicles.

The big prize for the longer-term future, though, would be a space vehicle propelled by nuclear fusion. When this technology is eventually developed, a large spaceship could be propelled at stupendous speed by the energy released by the fusion of light elements such as hydrogen, helium, and lithium into heavier reaction products. Even further off, and potentially even more powerful, is the possibility of the energy release produced by the combination and annihilation of matter and antimatter. Laser-pushed lightsails might also be used to power extremely light spacecraft using enormous amounts of power, though the economics of the enterprise would be crippling. A feasible manned spacecraft to reach the nearest stars would need a lightsail 600 miles (960 kilometers) across, would have to be assembled in the orbit of Mercury, and would need solar powered lasers delivering approximately 75,000 times the present total world output of power!

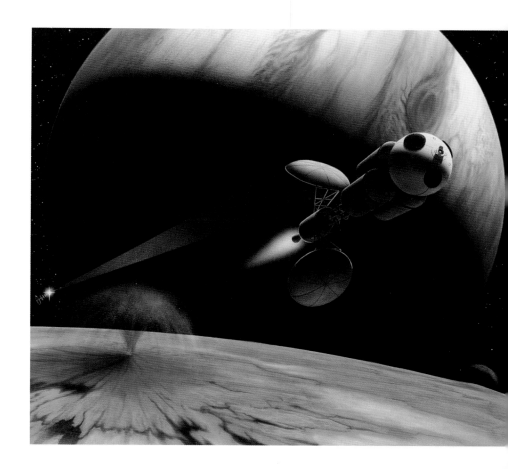

THIS PAGE
Bottom The connecting of the
Russian supply module Zarya
with Unity.
Below An imaginary space colony,
the concept for which was drawn
up as far back as 1975.

laboratory module developed by the European Space Agency. In all, 100,000 people are working on different parts of the ISS, and sixteen different nations are involved over the ten year program—the United States, Russia, Belgium, Brazil, Canada, Denmark, France, Germany, Holland, Italy, Japan, Norway, Spain, Sweden, Switzerland, and the U.K. The complete structure will weigh 460 tons and be completed by 2004, with thirty-three American shuttle flights and the launching of twelve Russian rockets. It will orbit Earth at an altitude of some 280 miles (950 kilometers) and a speed of 18,000 miles an hour (28,960 kilometers an hour), and its footprint will cover 85 percent of Earth's surface. A total of fifty-two computers will monitor its operations, and the total internal space will be similar to that of a Boeing 747.

Construction began with the launch of the Russian supply module Zarya on November 20, 1998. The United States then launched the node module Unity on December 4, 1998, after an anxious day's delay due to a power

week later. Construction is proceeding in Russia on the first accommodation module that is due to join the station in March 2000, after which the first crew of three astronauts will take up residence aboard the ISS. When complete, the station will have room for six or seven occupants, living in two accommodation modules with two storage modules and seven laboratories. It is fitted with the robot arm, larger than the one fitted to the Space Shuttle, which can move along a special track extending over the entire length of the station. Over the ten-year planned life of the station, a total of some 900 scientists will be able to conduct medical, material, and other experiments in the weightless conditions, together with a detailed program of study of Earth, the Sun, and the wider universe. The station's communications systems will use 386 processors that, because their electronic circuits are larger than more recently developed chips, they are less vulnerable to radiation or other damage, which might cause switches to trip spontaneously.

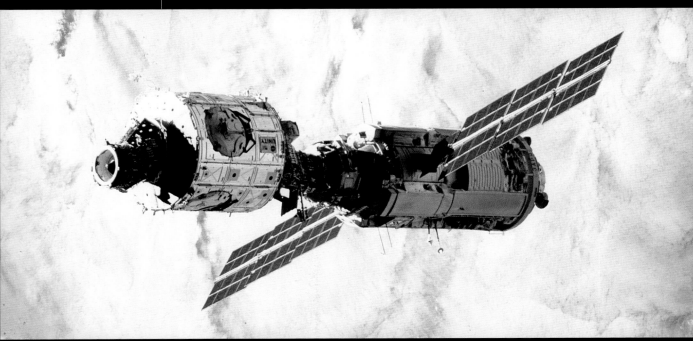

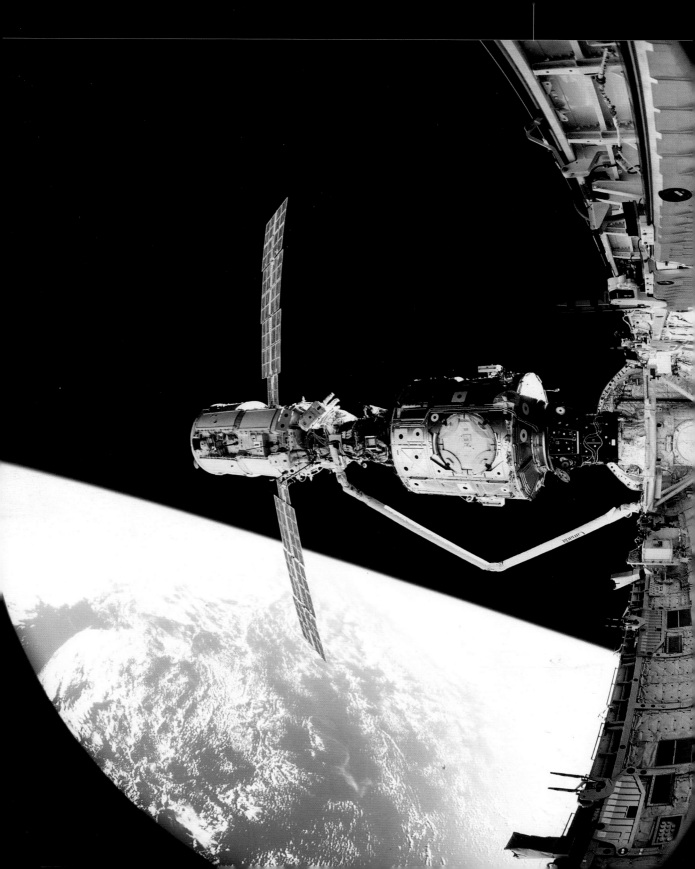

INDEX

PICTURE CREDITS

The publisher would like to thank the following for permission to reproduce their images. While every effort has been made to ensure this listing is correct the publisher apologizes for any omissions or errors.

NASA: pp 1, 2-3, 5, 14, 15, 16, 19, 22, 23, 24, 25, 26, 27, 32, 41(l), 51(t), 55, 64(r), 65(t), 67, 69(b), 70, 71, 76-87, 89-93, 94(t and b), 95, 96, 97, 99, 102-111, 114, 115, 118, 120, 121, 125, 126, 127, 129, 130(b), 131, 132-141

The Fotomas Index: p 9

Genesis Space Photo Library: pp 42, 44, 46, 47, 50, 53(l), 56(r), 60, 64(l), 65(b), 68, 88, 116, 117, 119, 122, 123, 124, 128, 130(t)

Fortean Picture Library: pp 28, 30 (bl, bc, br), 36, 37

Novosti Photo Library: pp 39, 48, 49, 51(b), 52, 54, 61(l), 62, 63, 100, 101, 112, 113

John Batchelor: pp 72, 73, 75

Science and Society Picture Library: pp 6, 7, 8, 10-13, 17, 18, 20, 21, 30(t), 40, 41(r), 43, 45, 53(r), 56(l), 57, 58, 59, 61(r), 66, 69(t), 74, 94(c)

British Film Institute: pp 29, 31, 35, 38

Marvel Comics: p 34(r)

DC Comics Inc: p 34(l)

BIBLIOGRAPHY

Exploring the Solar System, Nicholas Booth. Philip's, 1995.

Visions of Heaven: The Mysteries of the Universe revealed by the Hubble Space Telescope, Tom Wilkie and Mark Rosselli. Hodder & Stoughton, 1998.

Spacewatching: The Ultimate Guide to the Stars and Beyond, Dr John O'Byrne (Consultant Editor). HarperCollins, 1998.

The Cambridge Illustrated History of Astronomy, edited by Michael Hoskin. Cambridge University Press, 1997.

The Universe Revealed, edited by Pam Spence. Mitchell Beazley, 1998.

Planets (Smithsonian Guides), Thomas R. Watters. Macmillan USA, 1995.

The Giant Leap: Mankind Heads for the Stars, Adrian Berry. Hodder Headline, 1999.

The Space Race: Space Exploration Takes Off. Reader's Digest, 1999.

Countdown: A History of Space Flight, T. A. Heppenheimer. John Wiley & Sons, 1997.

One Giant Leap: The Extraordinary Story of the Moon Landings, Tim Furniss. Carlton Books, 1998.

All We Did was Fly to the Moon, Dick Lattimer. Whispering Eagle Press, 1985.

Echoes Among the Stars: A Short History of the U.S. Space Program, Patrick J. Walsh. M. E. Sharpe, 1999.

Exploring the Moon: The Apollo Expeditions, D M Harland. Springer Verlag, 1999.

NASA and the Exploration of Space, Roger D Launius, Bertram Ulrich, and John Glenn. Stewart, Tabori & Chang, 1998.

Spaceflight: a Smithsonian Guide, Valerie Neal. IDG Books Worldwide, 2000.

Where next, Columbus ? The Future of Space Exploration, edited by Valerie Neal. Oxford University Press, 1994.